THE PURPOSE OF THE STORM

Overcoming the Biggest Storm of My Life

Dr. Joseph O. Nipah

authorHOUSE®

AuthorHouse™ UK Ltd.
1663 Liberty Drive
Bloomington, IN 47403 USA
www.authorhouse.co.uk
Phone: 0800.197.4150

© 2014 Dr. Joseph O. Nipah. All rights reserved.

No part of this book may be reproduced, stored in a retrieval system, or transmitted by any means without the written permission of the author.

Published by AuthorHouse   03/11/2014

ISBN: 978-1-4918-9739-3 (sc)
ISBN: 978-1-4918-9738-6 (hc)
ISBN: 978-1-4918-9740-9 (e)

Any people depicted in stock imagery provided by Thinkstock are models, and such images are being used for illustrative purposes only.
Certain stock imagery © Thinkstock.

This book is printed on acid-free paper.

Because of the dynamic nature of the Internet, any web addresses or links contained in this book may have changed since publication and may no longer be valid. The views expressed in this work are solely those of the author and do not necessarily reflect the views of the publisher, and the publisher hereby disclaims any responsibility for them.

Most of the Scripture quotations are taken from the Holy Bible, New International Version (NIV) unless otherwise stated. Listed below are the sources of the versions used in this publication:

The Holy Bible, New International Version
Copyright © 1973, 1978, 1984, 2011 by Biblica, Inc. All rights reserved worldwide.

The Holy Bible, King James Version
Copyright © 1998-2014. By Olive Tree Bible Software

Good News Bible (GNB)
British usage edition first published 1976.
Good News Bible with introductory helps first published 1986.
The Bible Societies

Scripture quotations marked GNT are taken from the Good News Translation — Second Edition. Copyright © 1992 by American Bible Society. Used by permission. All rights reserved.

Scripture quotations marked NKJV are taken from the New King James Version. Copyright © 1982 by Thomas Nelson, Inc. Used by permission. All rights reserved.

DEDICATION

To God be the glory, for the great things He has done. I dedicate this book to my dear wife Evelyn for her love and support through the most challenging period of my life. I am eternally grateful to God for leading me into your life; you have been a true blessing. To my children Theophilus, Michelle and Kwame, who have had to endure extended periods of my absence from home in my professional and ministerial pursuits; I love you very much.

Contents

ACKNOWLEDGEMENTS viii

FOREWORD ix

Introduction 1

Chapter 1
God's promises and my struggles 7

Chapter 2
Health challenges 19

Chapter 3
The crucial decision 35

Chapter 4
My in-between period 53

Chapter 5
Treatments and help from above 61

Chapter 6
All working together for good 83

REFERENCES 97

Acknowledgements

I am very grateful to Dr Ezekiel and Dr (Mrs.) Funmi Alawale, the Senior Pastors of God's Vineyard Ministries, UK. You have been of great inspiration to me. Your leadership, balance and prayer lives stir me up always. The effective ways in which you manage the high demands of medical practice, ministry and family commitments have left great impressions in my life. I am grateful to God for your lives.

I am also grateful to the entire leadership of God's Vineyard Ministries for the opportunity given me to serve in the Master's Vineyard. The immense support from the leadership and congregation of the Loughborough branch of the church is deeply appreciated. I derive great inspiration from the team day after day. I value your input in my life.

I also pay special tribute to Bishop Ebenezer Sefah; the General Overseer of The Refreshing Hour International Church; whose drive, enthusiasm and encouragement paved the way for me to make a commitment into ministerial service.

I also thank Dr Femi Fenojo, Miss Esther Opiyo and Miss Angela Kahendeke who helped with editing of the manuscript. The cover and the lay out were originally designed by Ayo Oladeji. His contribution is greatly appreciated.

The wonderful support given me by my wife Evelyn is greatly appreciated. Finally, I would like to acknowledge the role of my children Theo, Michelle and Kwame, whose love and tenderness give so much meaning to my life. I pray for God to bless everyone who made this publication possible.

Foreword

God indeed rules in the affairs of all men. In particular, He determines the course of the lives of those who are fully surrendered to Him. This is the major truth that this book exemplifies. The story and admonition in this book also underscores God's sovereignty. It gives the reader the assurance that the Lord preserves the life of His saints.

On one hand, this is a story of a man who loves God and is passionate about the business of The Kingdom. On the other hand, it is a story of a man who was not only excited at the prospects of his career in scientific research, but was also committed to pursuing it. To the author, it did not make much difference whether he chose to live in Ghana, the place of his birth, or in the United Kingdom. There were platforms in either location to serve The Lord to the best of his ability; so he thought.

Settling in Ghana, to him, appeared to be the better option because it would have enabled him to pursue both his research career and God's calling on his life. Ghana also seemed to be the place to resettle and be happy; considering the initial challenges he had faced in the United Kingdom. However, as you will discover through this account, God has His perfect will for each one of us. As long as we cooperate with and do not rebel against Him, He will order our steps and chart our course into this perfect will.

Challenges and tough times in the life of a child of God can sometimes deal a dent in the confidence that the believer has in God's faithfulness. As you read this book, it becomes more obvious that often, God allows challenging circumstances in the lives of His children, in order to bring them to where He has ordained them to be.

The story of this servant of God, affectionately called Pastor Joe, is a classic example of what God can bring out of the stormy situations in the life of a believer. Whether it is a life threatening situation, as accounted in this book, or any other situation that is capable of destroying something in your life; God is able to use the same situation as a channel to bring you to His best intentions for your life. The Psalmist said:

> 'Thou hast caused men to ride over our heads; we went through fire and through water: but thou broughtest us out into a wealthy place' **(Psalm 66:12 KJV)**.

This account also highlights the truth; that things we cannot understand, or explain, could happen to a true believer in Christ. One thing to note, however, is that God does not leave us to go through them on our own; He walks with us to ensure that we are not destroyed by them. Isaiah 43:2-3 (GNB) says:

> 'When you pass through deep waters, I will be with you; your troubles will not overwhelm you. When you pass through fire, you will not be burned; the hard trials that come will not hurt you. For I am the LORD your God . . .'

As clearly demonstrated by this account, challenges in the lives of believers usually end up strengthening their faith; they usually become the basis for their testimonies. Having been through it all, one is able to look back with the benefit of hindsight; acknowledging its purpose and giving Glory to God.

> *'Every test that you have experienced is the kind that normally comes to people. But God keeps his promise, and he will not allow you to be tested beyond your power to remain firm; at the time you are put to the test, he will give you the strength to endure it, and so provide you with a way out'* **(1Corinthians 10:13 GNT).**

Another important outcome of the challenges Christians face is that it equips them to uphold others. The experiences the author has been through have undoubtedly equipped him to succour others who may be going through any experiences of similar magnitude. That indeed is the purpose of this book.

Pastor Joe has extraordinary grace; he is a bundle of great potential. Furthermore, he is a Kingdom-minded person; sold out for God. He and his family are a blessing to a countless number of people today, particularly the youth; and the best is yet to come!

God's faithfulness echoes through Pastor Joe's story. God is ever so faithful; He never fails. He is no respecter of persons. Just as He has done with Pastor Joe, He will do with anyone who truly loves Him and is called according to His purpose; the same and more.

> *'We know that in all things God works for good with those who love him, those whom he has called according to his purpose'* **(Romans 8:28 GNB).**

It is my personal conviction that when God went as far as He did to secure the life of Pastor Joe; He had the lives and destinies tied to His servant in mind. The greater the destinies God attaches to a life, the more He intervenes in the affairs of that life. Looking at it in another way; the more you choose to live to fulfil God's interests, the more you give God reason to fight for you. He will sustain you here on earth, because He needs you here. The apostle Paul said:

> *'I am pulled in two directions. I want very much to leave this life and be with Christ, which is a far better thing; but for your sake it is much more important that I remain alive. I am sure of this, and so I know that I will stay. I will stay on with you all, to add to your progress and joy in the faith'* **(Phil 1:13-25)**

God bless you as you read through this book. I pray He not only strengthens your faith, but also keeps you on course to fulfil the glorious destiny He has in store for you.

Dr. Ezekiel Alawale
(Senior Pastor: God's Vineyard Ministries)

INTRODUCTION

One of my greatest ambitions in life was to become a high flying research scientist. For that reason, in the early years after my graduation from the university, I ignored opportunities for other good jobs that did not involve research. I eventually got a job with the largest research council in Ghana, West Africa, where I was taken on as an Assistant Research Officer in the Council for Scientific and Industrial research (CSIR).

Over the years that followed, I saw my dream come through as I had opportunities to further my studies in reputable research institutions around the globe; including some research centres of the Consultative Group for International Agricultural Research (CGIAR) and the University of Nottingham, where I obtained a Master of Philosophy degree in Plant Breeding and a Doctor of Philosophy in Plant Sciences, respectively.

During those years, I was blessed with a wonderful wife and three lovely children. Meanwhile, I had also had opportunities to pursue part time courses in Biblical Studies and Christian Discipleship; and had been ordained as a Minister of Religion in the year 2000. I was passionate about my ministerial duties and did my best to serve my God through the opportunities He brought my way. While pursuing a career in the field of research, I had been deeply involved in ministry; I served as a resident pastor in a couple of churches in Ghana and in the United Kingdom.

Following my academic achievements, I had great opportunities to manage a number of high ranking collaborative research projects with reputable organisations including CIRAD-France, BBSRC-UK, Royal Society-UK, the University of Nottingham, etc. I had risen to the position of a Senior Research Scientist in the field of research and was clearly on my way to the top when without warning, the greatest challenge of my life struck. I was hit with the biggest storm of my life!

Well, the good news is that God's faithfulness saw me through; I survived to tell the story. This book is a narrative account of the biggest storm I have ever experienced. My objective for writing this account is to bring encouragement to those who love God and are called according to His purpose.

Through these experiences, one scripture that has become so meaningful to me is Romans 8: 28

> *'And we know that all things work together for good to them that love God, to them who are the called according to His purpose'.*

Through my own experiences, the experiences in the lives of other believers and consistent biblical examples; I have come to understand that storms do come the way of the believer, regardless of one's level of faith. Sometimes, such stormy times cause real havoc in the life of the Christian and their loved ones. On several occasions I have asked this question; 'why do bad things happen to good people'? If God is a loving Father as we are made to believe, why can He not simply keep His children from such storms of life? I suppose many of us have asked these questions too, but answers to these questions continue to elude us. For me, however, a clearer understanding of Romans 8:28 has provided an answer that more or less settles the issue.

The first emphasis the apostle Paul makes in this passage gives indication about the certainty of his knowledge. He said *<u>'and we know'</u>*; he did not say, we think or we feel or we can assume. The certainty conveyed by the phrase 'we know' could have its basis in something that had been proven by repeated occurrence. In other words, the phrase can relate to something that is the norm, rather than the exception. In effect, whatever he was about to say, which was preceded by that phrase was a familiar occurrence that they could all attest to. So what was it that they knew?

With those who love God and who are called according to His purpose; <u>all things</u> <u>work together for their good</u>.

As explained in my book 'The Hidden Power of Forgiveness', our lives as Christians are all about fulfilling divine purpose. For those who commit their lives, resources and energy to seeking and fulfilling this purpose that God has for them on this earth; God will work through every situation in their lives to ensure that they live to fulfil that purpose. It does not matter whether the situation is brought about by God Himself or it comes about as a result of the Devil's attack on their lives. It will not matter whether a situation in their lives was intended for good or for evil; God is able to use *<u>all</u>* circumstances in our lives to achieve His purpose. It is against this background that I will encourage you not to relegate God to the background in your life; it pays to be driven by the purpose for which He created you. Do not spend all your years on earth chasing after needs and pleasures that will never be gratifying regardless of how much you acquire. The plain truth is that no matter how dedicated you are to God, there will be bitter and happy moments in your life. What this scripture is saying is that God will bring both the good and the bad, or the sweet and the bitter experiences together, as recipes for a perfectly finished product. They are all necessary ingredients that **_work together_** to ensure an adorable finished product. For example, not all the individual ingredients in a tasty meal are tasty in themselves. While some individual ingredients could be consumed and enjoyed as single products, others may taste too spicy, sour or too bitter when taken on their own. However, when the individual ingredients are handed over to a skilful cook, they are able to put them together to produce a tasty meal, which is the end product everyone is interested in.

It is this truth that I intend to bring out through this story of my life to encourage the people of God. The lessons I learnt during the most vulnerable period of my life form the basis of the exhortations that are sandwiched between the narratives of the different phases of my experiences. I learnt among others that though *'weeping may endure for a night'*, the righteous need to be assured that *'joy comes in the morning'* (Psalm 30:5b). When God declared through the prophet Jeremiah to His people;

> *'I know the thoughts that I think toward you, saith the LORD, thoughts of peace, and not of evil, to give you an expected end'* **(Je 29:11)**; *they were in servitude.*

As you journey through this book with me, it is my prayer that you will be reminded of how God is able to use unimaginable channels to bring His intentions to pass in our lives. Your story may be different, but I will encourage you to read on. There are lessons in here that will certainly encourage everyone who trusts in the Lord our God.

CHAPTER 1

GOD'S PROMISES AND MY STRUGGLES

*You let men ride over our heads; we went through fire and
water, but you brought us to a place of abundance
(Psalm 66:12 NIV)*

In late 2003, alone in my room one afternoon I was drawn into a deeply agonising prayer, seeking God's face for direction regarding the next phase of my life. I was earnestly praying for God to clarify to me if indeed, He had a hand in bringing me to the United Kingdom. I am not quite sure for how long I prayed that afternoon, but it was an earnest outpouring of my heart to God. And on this very remarkable day of my life, the Lord spoke to me clearly. In summary, the Lord strongly impressed these words on my heart: 'DWELL IN THIS LAND FOR A WHILE AND I WILL ESTABLISH YOU AND BLESS YOU'. I do not make the expression 'God spoke to me' lightly; I had no doubt that this was a direct Word from God to me in my time of agony. Clearly, God had heard my cry for help and responded so lovingly to me. My mourning was instantly turned into dancing; I began worshipping and praising God with all of my heart. Ironically, considering the circumstances of my life at that time, the words I had just received from God did not seem to make much sense at the time.

I had considered the opportunity to travel to England to study for a Doctorate degree in Plant Sciences as a divine opportunity, with extremely high expectations. My family and

I had been living in our comfort zone, feeling quite fulfilled with the humble achievements we had made in our lives. I had been working as a full time research scientist in the Western Region of Ghana, with one of the institutes of the largest research organisation in the country—The Council for Scientific and Industrial Research. I had already attained a Masters degree in Plant Breeding, which was enough to get me to a descent position in the organisation. I had a good working knowledge in my field of expertise and was part of a hard working team that had won a couple of national awards for some innovative and pioneering research. I had on a number of occasions tried to secure funding to pursue a Doctorate degree, but I was unsuccessful. I had therefore accepted the fact that, my ambition to pursue a PhD degree may never materialise.

Additionally, I was deeply involved in Christian ministerial service; having been ordained as a Minister of Religion in the year 2000. I was then serving as one of the local pastors in the Headquarters branch of a Pentecostal church—The Refreshing Hour International Church in Sekondi-Takoradi, the administrative capital of the Western Region. I had also been helping in managing the Bible College of the ministry, as the Principal and Dean of Academic affairs. My wife was a registered Nurse/Midwife who was quite comfortable with her job. The Lord had blessed us with three wonderful children and we were loved and acceptance by our congregation and the community in which we lived. The church was great and the congregation loved our ministry.

On one occasion, the coordinator of my research team forwarded an announcement from the council's head office to me. It was for a postgraduate scholarship for which interested members of staff could apply. Among my colleagues, I was the only one who showed any interest. The problem however was that it was just a day to the deadline for the application to reach the head office; meanwhile it could take up to two weeks to put any meaningful proposal together with supporting documents. When I complained about the delay in the information getting to our unit, the coordinator got in touch with the head office and succeeded in getting them to extend the deadline for two more weeks, to make it possible for me to submit my application. I later learnt that I was the last person to submit my application, and I ended up being one of the few successful candidates. I was offered a scholarship to pursue a PhD degree in Molecular Biology in the field of Plant Sciences in any University of my choice. My first preference was a University in Australia, but some challenges in applying for a visa made it difficult to pursue that option. After a long discourse between scientists who were interested in my research proposal, I was finally admitted to the University of Nottingham to commence my studies in September 2003. This was a dream coming through for me. Indeed, it is the dream of many people in Africa to study in the West, particularly in England and the Unites States of America. I was therefore, obviously excited about the opportunity and was fully convinced that God was the reason behind it all.

However, not long after arriving in England, my excitement was very quickly dashed; I felt very lonely and isolated. My perception from previous visits to Europe for conferences was not what I was now experiencing, after settling in the community. I had travelled alone, without my family into a culture that was completely different from what I was used to. There was practically no social life for me. I could not survive on the meagre subsistence allowance I was receiving and had to supplement it by taking up agency jobs. I took up jobs I never dreamt of doing. My life revolved around my laboratory work at the University, part time jobs and a small church congregation I had found. I spent most evenings alone in my room.

Christmas that year was the worst I ever experienced. In Ghana, where I had come from, Christmas was a social event. The streets are usually filled with celebrants; where people would freely interact with others they do not know. Having been that lonely for three months, I looked forward to Christmas with great anticipation. I woke up on Christmas day expecting to see the streets packed. To my great disappointment, I stood looking through my window onto the streets for quite some time and I did not see one person pass. Suddenly, without control, I burst into tears; I cried like a baby. To make matters worse, I later learnt that buses do not run on both Christmas and Boxing days and stores were closed on Christmas day. I was totally unprepared for this experience; it was just too much for me to deal with.

It was these developments that led me to pray my heart out to God seeking clarification as to whether He had been involved from the beginning or it was simply me jumping on an opportunity thinking it was divinely given. If He could only convince me that I had missed it from the beginning, I suppose I would have seriously considered calling it quits at that time. I guess this will look familiar to many readers; we battle with questions when the going gets tough in our faith walk with God. In Scripture, John the Baptist is a classic example of a person who experienced wavering faith. John through the Holy Spirit, recognised the unborn Jesus as the Christ, while he was himself in his mother's womb (Luke 1:41-42). He had so much to say about Jesus before He began His public ministry (Luke 3:16). John was the first to point Jesus out as the Lamb of God who takes away the sin of the world (John 1:29). As a result of the deep revelation John had of Jesus and in the light of the miracles Jesus had been performing in the lives of even those who had no commitment to Him; when John ran into trouble, he obviously expected Jesus to show up and miraculously bring him out in a show of triumph. Having waited long enough without hearing from Him, John sent some of his disciples to ask Jesus;

> *"are you the one John said was going to come, or should we expect someone else?"* **(Matt 11:3 GNB)**.

Many of us have experienced moments where after triumphantly taking hold of divinely orchestrated opportunities, we encountered numerous challenges that made us wonder if God had indeed been there from the beginning. It may be a job opportunity, a relationship that began well, a conviction to give in support of God's work, a business partnership you were so sure of etc; which you are now having second thoughts about.

These experiences brought Isa 43:2-3 (GNB) very much alive to me. It says

> *'When you pass through deep waters, I will be with you; your troubles will not overwhelm you. When you pass through fire, you will not be burned; the hard trials that come will not hurt you. For I am the LORD your God, the holy God of Israel, who saves you'.*

I took note of the fact that God did not promise to remove the fire and the deep waters or the troubles before we get there. What He promised however was that He will be with us and ensure that those challenges do not destroy us. The circumstances of my life have enabled me to come to terms with the realisation that, the righteous may indeed go through challenging times, but if we can rely on God; He will be available to deliver us from ALL of them; Many are the afflictions of the righteous, but Jehovah delivers him out of them all. He keeps all his bones; not one of them is broken **(Ps 34:20-21a MKJV).** *I will have more to discuss on this in Chapter 3.*

Following that unique encounter, when God gave me that promise, things truly began to work out. My family was able to join me in January of 2004. It was one of the best things that happened to me since I had been in England. Before the journey, my wife had also received a confirmation from the Lord that He was with us and that He had plans for our lives. These notwithstanding, the arrival of my wife in England brought another twist to the whole story. She had taken three years leave of absence from her job back in Ghana hoping to gain professional experience in England that would give her some advantage by the time she gets back. For a long time, she could not find a job as a Nurse; she had to work as a line operative in a number of factories, standing on her feet for extended hours. She would cry almost every day and wished that our circumstances could have permitted us to go back home immediately. She was visibly unhappy at the turn of events in our lives; those who knew her would comment over and over that she looked unhappy.

This was a very difficult time for me because I knew there were more challenges ahead. What gave me great concern was that, my research was a sandwich programme; meaning that I had to do some aspects in England and some field based research back in Ghana. I had hoped my wife would quickly settle to give me the peace of mind to travel back to Ghana to commence my field research. Regardless of the uncertainties, six months after the family joined me; I had to relocate to Ghana with my two younger children, leaving my wife and my oldest son to pursue her job hunt for a registered nurse position. This was a very difficult decision to make, but it appeared to be the best of the choices available to us then. I spent most part of the next 15 months on the fields gathering data. On many occasions we would call up and cry together over the phone and pray together. After some time, she did manage to secure a placement that eventually led to her registration as a staff nurse. Following some very challenging further developments, which I would not want to bore the reader with; she finally began working at the Queen's Medical Centre campus of the Nottingham University Hospital's Trust as a band 5 registered nurse. Wow! Can you imagine the joy we shared and the hopes we had. She had the intention of gaining as much experience as she could, and calling it quits the very day I received my Doctorate degree so that we could head back to the land of our birth. Soon afterwards, the realities of the challenges she was up against in her demanding new position became apparent.

Up until this time, I had noted a trend; every step of the way had encountered one challenge or another. The challenges surfaced in different shades and forms. Our expectation of a restful three-year period in England for the family had completely eroded. We were simply enduring each day in anticipation of me successfully completing my studies for us to go back and settle in the zone of comfort that we were so used to back in Ghana; an experience we had now come to appreciate very much. The promises of God to establish me in England had become irrelevant. The only thing on my mind was to complete my studies successfully and get out of the harsh conditions we had been enduring; a view my wife shared wholeheartedly.

Having completed my field research, the family was happily reunited in England in late 2005. I then began searching for a job to supplement our household income. For some reason, none of the organisation I applied to, got back to me except one. I was so desperate for a job and I was prepared to do anything that my visa would permit me to do. I came across an advertisement for a domestic assistant's position, which simply meant a cleaner, in one of the guest houses of the University. Not long after applying for the position, I received a response in a letter that read along these lines *'Dear Mr Nipah, thank you very much for your recent application for the position of a domestic assistant. We regret to inform you that quite a number of people who applied for the position, had more experience than you. Your application was therefore unsuccessful. We wish you a better luck next time'.* You can imagine how I felt. You will also appreciate why by this stage, any promise God had given to establish me in this same land that threatened to strip me of the hard earned dignity, which I had built over the years, had become completely irrelevant in all respects.

During that time, I was one day travelling with the Senior Pastor of God's Vineyard Ministries, the church which I had become a part of since I arrived in Nottingham since 2003. Without discussing what I was going through with him, he asked if I would be happy to do some hours in the church office each week for a small monthly allowance. I knew there was a lot of work that needed to be manned in the church office, but the money was not attractive. I assured him I will give it a thought and get back to him. I discussed with my wife and we decided to take it up; most probably out of the need and not so much for Christian commitment. It was what followed this decision that amazed me. Soon after I had affirmed my readiness to help with the work in the church office, responses to the applications I had previously made and had not heard anything from began coming in; offering me jobs which obviously promised better remuneration. Wow! Why did they wait till now? I asked myself. I then began struggling with the decision to take up the role in the church office. One evening, during a joint prayer session in church, I knelt down in a corner and ignored the prayer points being raised from the altar. I just poured my heart out asking God to guide me in making the right decision. While I was in prayer, whenever my mind inclined towards taking up the secular job, I felt some deep unrest in my heart; but when I thought to ignore those offers and commit to work in the church, I sensed real peace come over me. When this happened for the second time during the course of the prayer, I just threw in the towel and submitted my will to what I knew God wanted me to do.

The next day, I reported to the church office and began a 20 hour shift. This fitted very well with my school schedule, since at this stage, I was doing more writing on my thesis than laboratory work. With the benefit of hind sight, today I thank God for leading me in making that decision; this was later to play a significant role in fashioning the course of my life and to fulfil what unknown to me, God was setting me up for.

Following this decision, things appeared to be falling in place. A series of positive developments took place to set the stage for what was to come. I wholeheartedly committed to the roles I was assigned to and was later asked to pastor a new branch of the ministry in Derby, which was about 30 minutes drive from Nottingham. This role gave me great fulfilment and I enjoyed the full support of my family. Soon after celebrating the first anniversary of the Derby church, I was awarded my long awaited Doctorate degree in Plant Sciences in December 2007.

In the mean time, some months before my graduation, the Biotechnology and Biological Sciences Research Council (BBSRC) of the United Kingdom announced some significant amounts of money available to support collaborative research between institutions in the UK and the developing world. My main supervisor for my PhD research called me and discussed the prospects of putting in an application. We noted that with my experience and links with the CSIR in Ghana, we had a head start in securing funding if we could put together a good proposal. The area I had been researching into was quite innovative and we were able to develop some comprehensive follow up research, which my supervisor and I were to co-investigate. It was included in the terms of the project that I was to be a co-investigator who was to lead the field research involving field data collection in Ghana. Samples collected were then to be sent over to the laboratories in the United Kingdom for analysis. The project was spiced with a number of visits both to Ghana and the UK by the research team. To our great delight, our application was successful and just in time to make my impending journey to Ghana more imminent.

There was however, another positive twist of events. Around this time when I was drawing down the curtain on my sojourning in the UK, prospects for my wife relocating to her field of interest in nursing to gain more expertise became real. She had been working in the orthopaedic unit, but being a midwife, she had hoped to gain some experience in gynaecology. This trend of events was paramount in our decision to leave the family in England while I move to Ghana to commence my highly reputable BBSRC-funded project. My wife subsequently succeeded in relocating to the gynaecology unit and had offers to enrol in the University of Nottingham for a Degree in Nursing with a special focus on sexual health. Her nursing qualification from Ghana at the time she graduated was at a certificate level. These offers were therefore not to be missed.

As a result of these developments, we mutually agreed for her to remain in the UK, while I and the two younger children move back to Ghana. Our oldest child was to remain in England with my wife because of the level he had reached in his education. We had always been concerned about the disruption his education would suffer when we returned to Ghana. So now that he had the option to continue in the UK, we decided for him to carry on. Besides, my wife was happy to have a much needed companion while the rest of us were away.

My story so far could very well be summarised in the scripture *'You let men ride over our heads; we went through fire and water, but you brought us to a place of abundance'* **(Psalm 66:12 NIV).**

Soon afterwards, I began my post qualification research activities. I travelled the length and breadth of the fields of Ghana collecting samples. Though I spent most of those days outside the United Kingdom, we had by this stage decided to maintain our base in the UK until my wife had completed her Nursing degree. I used to travel in and out of the UK for project activities and to be with the family. This arrangement continued until, without warning, a sudden shocking occurrence struck like a thunderbolt that turned the tide of my entire life in a completely different direction.

CHAPTER 2

HEALTH CHALLENGES

You need not fear any dangers at night or sudden attacks during the day or the plagues that strike in the dark or the evils that kill in daylight (Psalm 91:5-6 GNB).

In early 2008, I travelled back to Ghana to commence my new role on the BBSRC project. My excitement about my work was demonstrated through the enthusiasm with which I went about my day to day activities; I maintained very active daily schedule. My usual daily routine involved jumping out of bed early for a time of devotion and running around throughout the day; crossing over from the fields to the laboratory, doing cross country travels along difficult terrains, doing school rounds with the kids, crossing over to church or to the Bible School, and on and on until I retire to bed, usually quite late. I also tried to maintain a healthy lifestyle; trying hard to do some basic exercises each morning or evening. My only major health challenge was battles with malaria, which doctors in that part of the world do not really consider a big deal.

Then, all of a sudden, I began experiencing a number of health challenges. I began losing weight; I lost significant weight within a short time, but I did not personally notice it till people began making comments about my looks. The wife of my senior pastor in Ghana travelled to the United States of America for two month and returned to remark that I had lost too much weight. I did not really make a big deal out of it. My normal body weight had been 72 Kg. I thought that the sudden change in my daily routine, which was physically quite demanding was the reason for any observable weight loss. But when another person made the same comment, I became a bit more concerned. Later when I checked, I had dropped down to 64 Kg in weight.

The next remarkable observation I made towards the end of 2008 was a feeling of tightness under my feet. On getting out of bed, my soles felt as if they were slightly swollen on touching the floor. This was only a feeling; I could not observe anything visible on close observation, so I simply ignored it and carried on with my usual schedule. Sometime in February 2009, however, I noted that my ankles were swollen. My daughter noticed it as well; when she pressed into it, the depression remained for some time before levelling up. The swellings caused me some level of pain around the joints. I knew then that there was something wrong somewhere within my body. I quickly booked to see my doctor, who queried gout as a possible diagnosis or a reaction from a sulphur-based drug, which I had taken earlier to treat malaria. This was treated with medication including some strong pain reliefs.

Thirdly, from late February through the entire period of March that same year, I experienced a cough that would just not stop. I took all the medications the doctor prescribed; it just wouldn't go away. My 45th birthday was coming up in March, and my wife had come down from England for a big celebration. I had never really celebrated my birthday with a big party; it had always been a small family affair. For some reason, I began thinking that the 45th milestone was significant. I therefore brought together friends and family to celebrate my life with a big cocktail party.

By May of that year, I began feeling some painful sensation on the left floor of my mouth close to my neck. I reported the development to my doctor, who initially suspected that it may have something to do with tonsillitis; which is an inflammation of the tonsils of the mouth, caused either by bacteria or a virus, which makes the throat very sore and can lead to fever and earache. When the pain persisted after a couple of visits to the clinic, the doctor referred me to a private Ear, Nose and Throat specialist, who could not make any meaningful diagnosis from the symptoms. By late May, I could now clearly feel a swelling slowly developing in the area where the pain was localised. The pain was particularly excruciating after I had preached in church. By this stage, I was constantly on pain reliefs both prescribed and self administered; I could hardly bear the pain without them.

I became very concerned about the sudden deterioration in my health, but it appeared medical personnel had no answers to what was going on in my body. I could hardly sleep without pain killers. The pain had now affected the sensation along the left side of my tongue; it felt numb and thick saliva constantly filled that side of my mouth. I knew then that I was in deep trouble; but I could not figure out what it was.

I prayed and prayed extensively for God to come to my rescue, but the pain persisted. However, on Sunday the 5th of July, 2009 something remarkable happened. My Satellite TV had been on God's Channel; one moment, I came through the living room just in time to hear the evangelist Benny Hinn giving a word of knowledge or a prophetic declaration along these lines: *'There is someone watching me now, who needs to administer the Holy Communion to himself for seven consecutive days'.* I was desperate for divine intervention, so I instantly decided to key into it and do it for myself, whether this was a message from God specifically to me or not. I was moving on out of the hall when I heard him add *'I am speaking to someone dealing with a cancer'.* That almost dissuaded me from carrying on with my plans to administer the Holy Communion to myself, because I could not be dealing with cancer. In effect, I concluded on the basis of his last statement that the message was certainly for someone else; regardless, I decided to still do it, trusting that God will come to my rescue by that act.

It was a Sunday morning, and I was preparing to travel the next day on a project assignment. Towards the evening of that same day, reports reached us that there had been a heavy storm in a town where one of our local churches was located. A few of the leaders of the church were quickly mobilised to travel to the affected area to see the victims and to provide some urgent supplies to support them. A church service was quickly organised by the local pastor for us to have the opportunity to meet all the members. On the way, I was asked if I could share something from scripture to encourage the church during the meeting. The only message that dropped on my heart was on *'the brevity of life'*, which made such a big impact on the lives of the members. Looking back today, this could well have been a message to prepare me for death, which was imminently staring me in the face without my knowing. The next morning, I came through the church premises and took some Holy Communion packs on my way to the official assignment. Every evening for the next seven days, in my hotel room, I would pray for an extended period and then administer to myself the Holy Communion. At the end of the seven days, the pain was intact; it had not diminished and the lump that had developed under my tongue could now be felt from both outside and inside of the left side of my mouth.

With the benefit of hindsight, I thank God for that intervention because I believe it played a very significant role in saving me from imminent death. I later linked this development to a dream I had around that same time, in which I saw an outstretched arm with a solid rock-like object in the palm. At the time, I could not make any meaning out of it, but on one fateful afternoon, when the Lord flashed that view back to me, I remembered my dream and praised God for His ever present grace and mercy. I will allude to this later where it all came together to make sense to me.

By this stage, I had lost any hope of finding a medical solution in Ghana, so I decided not to visit the clinic any more. My only hope was to pray for God to help me out. In August of that year, an important peer review meeting was scheduled to bring all research workers on the BBSRC project together in Nottingham. So I had it in mind to consult my GP on arrival back in Nottingham; hoping to gain some understanding into what was happening to me. On the day I was travelling, I was in so much pain. I visited a pharmacy shop to purchase some pain relief and if possible some antibiotics. The pharmacist however refused to prescribe the antibiotics after learning that doctors had already put me on them. After listening to my story, she suggested I could also see my dentist, because it could have something to do with that. With this, I called my wife to book an appointment with my Dentist in Nottingham;

she secured a booking for the next day after my arrival in the UK.

The dentist made a number of observations, including some x-rays and concluded that the pain had nothing to do with my teeth or the tonsils. He could however not make any diagnosis. It was at this stage that he made the decision to refer me to the Maxillofacial Unit of the Queen's Medical Centre (QMC), the hospital where my wife had been working since her registration as a Staff Nurse. While my official meetings and laboratory visits were going on, I was invited by the maxillofacial team to undergo some observations. What I had hoped to be a simple observation turned out to go on and on. I was booked for various scans, which initially included Ultrasound scan, where a biopsy (or a sample) was taken from the area where the pain was localised for laboratory analysis. A fine needle and syringe was inserted into the area to take a sample for analysis.

I was also booked to undergo a CT (computerised tomography) scan. Upon further enquiry, I learnt that the CT scan is a sophisticated type of x-ray, which builds up a detailed three-dimensional picture of the inside of the body, which could help the medical expert determine what exactly was happening in the area of concern.

While this process was going on, my scheduled time to return to continue with some time-bound field research activities back in Ghana had elapsed and I was getting very concerned. I informed the members of my research team about the delay and we had to make alternative arrangements for some researchers back in Ghana to hold the fort for me.

When the two scans failed to give conclusive diagnosis, the consultant informed me that the most sensible thing to do was to surgically remove the lump, which was quite obvious by that stage. This was quite heavy to take in because up until this time, I had never been hospitalised in my entire lifetime. My concern was even more aroused when he explained the possible risks associated with such an operation. However, considering the pain I had been putting up with, the assurance of getting the problem sorted once for all was somehow welcome news.

So on Monday, the 23rd of November, 2009 I was admitted to the Ear Nose and Throat Ward C-24 of the Queen's Medical Centre (QMC) to undergo a surgical operation under general anaesthesia. The operation, which according to the medical team took about four hours, was successful (see pictures in plate 1). Later that evening in the ward, the senior consultant came to my bed side and informed me that **it was a big rock-solid lump**, which was difficult to get out. Later upon enquiries, I was told the size was {3.5 x 3.5 x 2} cm^3. He also added that he could not locate some nerves and was afraid I may have some permanent level of numbness on the left side of my tongue. He quickly added *'I believe the problem has been solved and there will be no need to do anything further'*. Anything, further! I wondered. I honestly did not understand what he had in mind, after implying that there could be the need to do anything beyond what I had already been through that day.

Most significantly, however, the moment he mentioned that what he took out was a big rock-solid lump, the picture in the dream I had earlier referred to, in which a solid rock-like mass was being held in the palm of an outstretched arm flashed back in my mind. Wow! Was God showing me then what He had planned to do now? This certainly took me back thinking about those days. I had prayed and prayed, but God appeared to do nothing about the excruciating pain I was enduring day after day. All I saw was a dream that seemed to have no bearing with what I was going through; only to have it flashed back to me after several months just in time to clarify the thoughts He had for me. He had indeed figured it all out! ***When I was down to nothing*** and I thought He had given no regard to my pain, ***He was up to something*** regarding my case. Regardless of this realisation, I still could not figure out the role the Holy Communion could have played in this process. I kept all these thoughts to myself.

I was discharged after two days in the Ward. Soon after the operation, the pain I had endured for well over seven months had vanished, to my great relief. I had informed my research colleagues that everything had gone well and I was looking forward to returning soon to continue with my project activities. My youngest son had been living with the family of the senior pastor of the church in Ghana longer than I had originally arranged and I was eager to see him. By this time, I had been away from my son for about four months.

After the procedure, I was booked for a number of follow up visits to the maxillofacial clinic to be sure the healing was progressing fine. Life felt really good and I looked forward to leaving the struggles of the past months behind me to make the best of the opportunities ahead. I was totally unprepared for what was to follow.

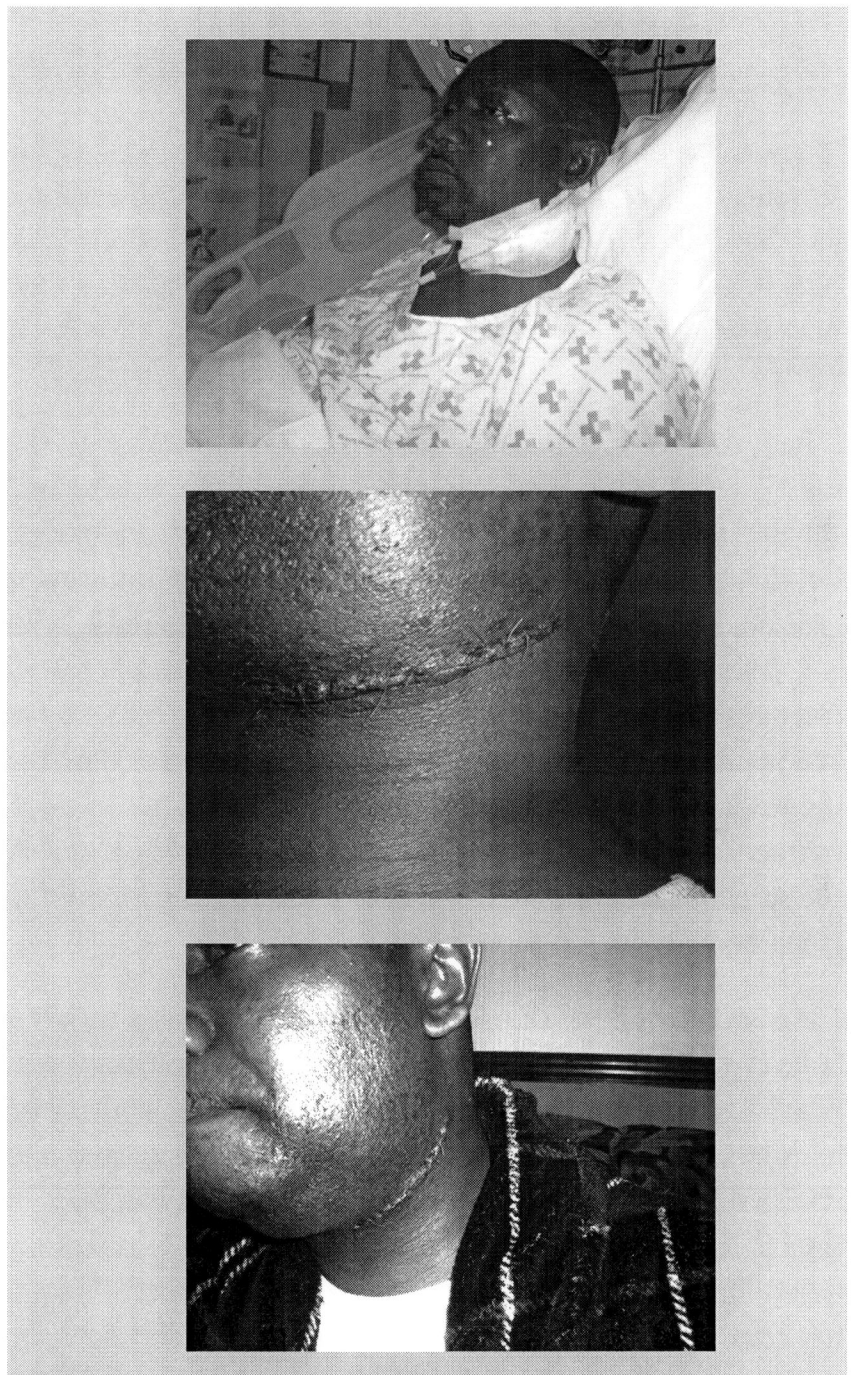

PLATE 1: *The immediate aftermath of the first operation*

THE BOMBSHELL

It was Wednesday the 2nd of December: the birthday of my youngest son, who was still in Ghana. I had called earlier to wish him a happy birthday. Obviously he had expected me to be back by this time and I had to explain that I needed to sort out some health issues and that it wasn't going to be long before I was back.

I had the second routine follow up appointment at the maxillofacial clinic. Following the surgery, the wound had suffered an infection, which had been treated with antibiotics. On this appointment, I was hoping to get the thumbs up to give me the liberty to plan my trip back to continue with my field research activities. A lot of perishable laboratory consumables had been packaged for me to take back to the labs in Ghana, and my concern at this stage was to ensure that the work did not stall. I had gotten in touch with my research partners at the University of Nottingham and told them that the surgery had gone well, and that I was looking forward to going back to the job soon.

I was seen by one of the doctors who I learnt was a registrar (a level just below a consultant). He was very pleasant and when he found out that I was Ghanaian and was working on a project that takes me back there, he was very excited and revealed that he was also Ghanaian by birth, but had been in the UK for a very long time. We spoke about family and many more. He made me feel quite relaxed as he flipped through my files. Then with commendable sense of composure, he gently released the bombshell!!! He said, *Joseph, I'm sorry but unfortunately, the results from the laboratory test done on the sample taken from the lump came back with further concern; the lump was diagnosed as* **Submandibular Gland Salivary Duct Adenocarcinoma**'. I did not understand what he was talking about. What does it mean? I asked. Then he said, *'it's a cancer; a rare type of cancer. We are not sure what causes it. There isn't much data to link it to a particular lifestyle; it affects smokers and non smokers alike . . . .'* He kept on and on but I don't remember hearing anything more. My thoughts were racing everywhere.

When I managed to pull myself together, I asked, 'so what is to be done about it?' Still very calm, he explained further that unfortunately, what they took out was a high grade cancer. I came to understand later that there are two grades of cancers; low and high grades. In high-grade cancers, the cells are said to look very abnormal under the microscope and are likely to grow quite quickly; they have higher tendency to affect other tissues and organs. This was the type they found. He therefore indicated that there is likely to be further treatment. He quickly added that the decision lies with the senior consultant; he could decide on a number of possible treatment pathways. He could simply decide that since the lump had already been taken out, we could just wait and see what happens. I later gathered that this option would have meant there is probably nothing more they felt could be done to save my life. The other options could be another operation or a regime of radiotherapy or both. He indicated further that the consultant will discuss my situation at the Head and Neck Multidisciplinary Team (MDT) meeting coming up the following week. After that, they will get in touch to let me know what the next line of action will be.

During the consultation, a lady up until this time appeared to be doing her own thing over a shelf on the other side of the consulting room. She was then introduced to me as a nurse specialist, who would take over from the registrar to give me the necessary support. She then took me to another office and offered some counselling support and some relevant literature on cancer. She promised to see me when I come back to meet with the consultant.

MY INITIAL REACTIONS

In the course of the consultation with the registrar, a number of questions were racing through my mind and I'm not sure to what extent I was concentrating on what he was saying. I wondered whether I was going to live or if this was it. What about my children, can my wife cope? How was I going to disclose this information to her? What about my project? Why me? Where did this come from . . . . ? The initial shock was obvious but I remained calm and reasonably composed. Somehow, deep within me, I had the conviction that God must have a reason to allow this to happen to me.

On my way to the clinic, I had parked my car at a Park and Ride to board a free bus to the hospital. The specialist nurse asked if I was OK to go home by myself, and I said yes. In the bus back to where my car was parked, more questions kept flooding my thoughts, but the question I struggled with the most was how to break the news to my wife. The reality of her youngest son celebrating his birthday without any of us being there had affected her mood already and I wasn't prepared to make it worse for her. More significantly, she was beginning a three-night duty from that same evening at work and it was too late for her to give any excuse not to be able to cover the shift. I thought it wise, therefore, to keep it to myself. I would wait until she was done with the shifts before breaking the news to her. The only challenge was whether I could maintain a positive front for three days without her noticing any change in my composure.

As soon as I got to my car, I picked up my phone and called Dr Ezekiel Alawale, the senior pastor of our church. I asked if he could kindly come over, giving him a time when my wife would have left for work. He did not hesitate for a moment before agreeing to come over later in the night. Following the telephone conversation, I sat down quietly in my car for a while, and out of the many issues that were racing through my mind for answers, at least I made two firm decisions. The first was to give up the project; there was no question about that. Secondly, much more importantly, I decided to bring my family together. Nothing else mattered to me than to have my family with me. I did not care about losing a job, money, property or friends; absolutely nothing mattered to me except my family. Rick Warren captured this feeling very well in his book 'The Purpose Driven Life'. He says *'I have been at the bedside of many people in their final moments, when they stand on the verge of eternity, and I have never heard anyone say, "Bring me my diplomas! I want to look at them one more time. Show me my awards, my medals, that gold watch I was given". When life on earth is ending, people don't surround themselves with objects. What we want around us is people—people we love and have relationship with. In our final moments we all realize that relationships are what life is all about. Wisdom is learning that truth sooner rather than later'.*

After a moment of very deep thought, I drove off and got home with no outward signs of what was going on within me. My wife obviously asked how it went and I only said something along the lines 'well, they are happy about the recovery process so far'. She was happy with that answer and so she went off to work with little concern about my condition. When Pastor Ezekiel later came over to my house, I opened up to him. Pastor Ezekiel is a man of prayer and of great faith in God. He had himself faced very serious challenges in life, and had experienced the power of prayer in turning situations around. Typical of him, after listening to my account, the first thing he said was 'it is well'! If the situation was a source of worry to him, he did not show it. He maintained his composure and assured me that he will be praying along with me and he was sure that God will sort it all out.

The next few days were very difficult to manage. Usually from a night shift my wife would have a shower, have some light breakfast and jump straight into bed; particularly if she was to go back to work that evening. During this time, however, she would come back from work and do her best to try and keep me company. But the longer she stayed around me, the more I felt tempted to tell her what was going on. While she was concerned about my recovery from the operation, I was more worried about how she was going to take the news I had just received. It was not easy to remain my usual self. I avoided looking her in the eyes; it could easily bring tears into mine. I somehow managed to keep the information to myself until Saturday.

On Saturday morning, she came back relieved that the long haul of duty was over. She was in a highly chatty mood and was not planning to go to bed as she was not working that evening. I waited for her to finish her breakfast. With my heart thumping, I managed to mutter the words, 'darling, sit down; I have something to tell you.' My wife knows me very well, and she knows when our conversation is no more casual. She knew something sensitive or very important was coming. That statement prodded her curiosity. She asked 'what!!!? Have they called you this morning? Is there any new development?' She was looking searchingly into my eyes as if to say, I have been through a lot already, please don't tell me there is more! I simply said, 'well, calm down and sit down'. She did, still with her eyes firmly fixed into mine. 'Well, unfortunately they have told me the lump was malignant, and I will need to undergo further treatment'. My wife hit her chest and shouted, J-E-S-U-S!!! Then she burst into uncontrollable tears. Our two older children were still asleep upstairs and I tried in vain to use that to calm her down. I was trying hard to convince her that the children must not be told at this stage and so she had to compose herself. It was to no avail; she could no longer sleep and wept throughout the whole day, staying away in the bedroom to keep away from the children. I was moved by her reaction, but I resolved to stay on top of the situation and not become emotional about it. Later that evening, when I explained my plans to bring back our last born son immediately, it gave her some consolation. Later that night she told me I had shocked her by managing to keep this information to myself for three days, and succeeded in pretending that everything was normal. I took advantage of that comment to crack light jokes about it and take our minds off the serious questions confronting us, which we had no answers to.

CHAPTER 3

THE CRUCIAL DECISION

The LORD says, "I will teach you the way you should go; I will instruct you and advise you. Don't be stupid like a horse or a mule, which must be controlled with a bit and bridle to make it submit"
(Psalm 32:9)

THE CONSULTATION

On my last visit to the maxillofacial clinic, I had been told that the MDT was to discuss my case on the following Thursday morning. As a result, I had been booked to come in late afternoon on Thursday to see the senior consultant. On Wednesday, the 9th of December, I had embarked on a day's fast to pray; which was more or less a routine exercise, but I took advantage of it to pray regarding the way forward. During the course of the day, I received an unexpected call from the secretary of the consultant asking if I could come to meet with the consultant that afternoon. I confirmed that my appointment was for the next day after the MDT meeting, but she explained that the consultant wanted to see me before the MDT meeting. So I agreed to come over before the clinic closes. She finally suggested that it would be prudent to come with a close relative or a friend. I dropped the phone. Hmm! What was it again? The good thing was that my wife had not returned to work and was available to accompany me. My experience that day is one I will never forget. I was told things I had never dreamt of happening to me. It was simply unthinkable.

There were probably about five or more medical staff in the consulting room with the senior consultant. After offering us seats, he came out straight without mincing words about what he intended to do. He bluntly explained that as a result of the nature of the malignant cells found in the lump, he had to conduct a second major operation to remove most of the glands and nodes from the affected side. He explained further that the rationale behind the second operation was that some tissues surrounding the lump may have been affected; and since there is no way of knowing which ones may have been affected, a lot had to be removed to reduce the chances of any cells growing out of control again. He said the operation would remove portions from the floor of the mouth and possibly a portion of the tongue if necessary.

By this stage, I was simply shaking my head as if to say, no! No!! No!!! He continued saying, the operation is big and may affect eating and drinking. He added that it could also affect my speech. At that moment, I interrupted and asked to what extent it could affect my speech. He answered saying he cannot guarantee anything; people react differently. Some struggle to speak but others recover their speech to a large extent. He added that in the event of difficulties, there are speech therapists available to assist those who end up with difficulties with their speech; so that they can be heard and understood. At that moment, something snapped in my heart. I straight away responded; 'thank you sir for your expertise but I don't want another operation.' It was at this point that I revealed to him that, beside my research experience, I was a preacher and that my fulfilment in life was linked to my speech. For that reason, I would not submit to any procedure that has the slightest possibility of leading to the loss of my speech. I made him aware that since the initial operation, which was comparatively minor, I had not even fully recovered the use of my tongue. I had developed a temporary lisp, which is a minor speech difficulty in which the sounds '*s*' and '*z*' are pronounced like the '*th*' sound, like a small child whose front teeth have not come through yet. In reaction to that, he looked me straight in the face and said, 'I have not said I will take your speech from you; what I have said is that your speech could be affected'. He then went on to reveal that he had successfully done the operation for a number of professionals, including a lecturer and a teacher who had both returned to their work.

With the issue of speech clarified, he went ahead to explain further details of what else the operation were to involve should we decide to go ahead with it. As the procedure could affect eating and drinking; before the main operation, he was intending to liaise with the nutrition department to first have a minor procedure done to place a feeding tube (PEG tube) through the abdominal wall into my stomach. This was to aid in feeding during the phases of the treatment when I will be unable to use my mouth either for drinking or eating or both. When I enquired how long the feeding tube could be in place, he confirmed it could be up to six months. I muttered to myself; Hah! Six months, with a tube hanging from my tummy!! No way; not me!!! The more he explained what he intended to do, the more I resolved that another operation was definitely not an option for me.

By this stage in the consultation, the full realisation of what I was dealing with began to dawn on me. I knew very little about cancer and what it took medically to remove or reduce the chances of reoccurrence. It was just too much to take in. Incidentally my wife was more relaxed about the information and I understood then why I was asked to come along with a close relative or a friend. There was just too much to process. Being a nurse, she apparently was familiar with the issues related with some types of cancer and she asked a number of questions about the feeding tube. I was just grim faced, with what I may refer to as 'holy anger' rising from inside me. I felt I did not deserve this. I had done my best to be a good Christian, and I was dedicated to God and to His work. Naturally speaking, I am not an evil person; I will go out of my way to help others. Why me? I guess most people reading this book would have asked such questions at some point in their lives.

Surprisingly the consultant was not put off by my reaction, which was by then, obvious to everyone in the room. He carried on with a high level of professionalism explaining what exactly will be happening on the operating table if I decided to go ahead with the 'big operation'. He then revealed yet another shocker: He explained that usually, due to the invasive nature of the procedures involved, there could be swellings in the region that could block the wind pipes during the recovery period. So the first thing he will be doing after putting me to sleep under general anaesthesia is making a hole in my neck and inserting a tracheostomy, through which I will be breathing. The procedure would involve making an incision in the front of the neck and opening a direct airway through the incision into the trachea or wind pipe. A tracheostomy tube will then be inserted into the resulting opening to allow me to breathe without the use of my nose or mouth. He added that during the early stages following the operation, the type of tube that will be inserted will not permit me to talk, because there will be no air going over the voice box. When he saw the reaction on my face, he quickly added that it was going to be a temporary situation, which could last for about two weeks, and that I will be given a note book to write what I would want to say at any point in time during the period.

He then asked me to stretch my hands towards him with my palms facing upwards. He felt the inner part of my wrist and asked if I was left or right handed. When I said I was right handed, he took my left hand and said the skin here is good for reconstruction. He educated that there are two major blood vessels that feed the palm. As a result of the tissues that are potentially going to be removed from the floor of the mouth, there will be the need to reconstruct the left side of the mouth covering the lower jaw. It was then that he made me understand that he will be taking a flap together with one of the blood vessels that feed the palm, and connecting them to other vessels in the neck area. The skin taken from my wrist will be grafted onto the site to close up the space created in my mouth. When he said that; once again something snapped in me! I said to myself; 'if you allow yourself to go through this, it will just finish you, Joe.' I looked over to my wife, and in all honesty, I thought I would be better of dying than go through what had just been unfolded to me. The consultant concluded that he needed to let me have the full picture; there was no need playing it down. Then he added that after the operation he was still going to recommend that I go through radiotherapy treatment. Having said that, he pulled his chair back a little, and gestured as if to say, now I am ready to listen to what you have to say.

MY RESOLUTE REACTION

I thanked him for his expertise and for taking the time to explain the process in detail to me. Then arrogantly, I added with some emphasis 'But I am sorry; I don't want another operation. I will be fine with radiotherapy, but certainly not another operation; I don't want it!' I did not know what radiotherapy involved and how intense it would be, but whatever it was, as long as it did not involve opening me up again; I thought I will be fine with it.

It was at this stage that it occurred to me that there were other people in the consulting room, with all eyes fixed on me. I was in my own world; I didn't care about what anybody was thinking. The consultant said 'Well, I don't want to do another operation, but I need to let you be aware that the malignant tumour we took out was high grade and whatever needs to be done, must be done sooner, rather than later to give you any chance of living'. He went further; 'I am blunt when it comes to this because there is no easy way around it. Even radiotherapy is not an easy option as you may suppose. Tomorrow I will be discussing your case at the MDT and I wanted to know your decision before then. I can give you time to go and think about it but my recommendation to the MDT will be an operation, as I have just explained to you, to be followed with radiotherapy. I will let them understand how you feel about it though.' I just didn't care anymore. I thought to myself, they can do all the deliberations they want; I am just not going for it. To end the consultation, he finally said,

'I am giving you two weeks to think carefully about all that I have said. If you come back to say you don't want to do it, I will not be offended, but I want you to think carefully about it'. In the mean time, he arranged for me to undergo a chest X-ray and MRI scan to be certain that the bad cells had not spread anywhere else.

One of the medical personnel in the doctor's consulting room was the specialist nurse, whom I had met the previous week when I was first told that I was dealing with a cancer. The consultant once again called her and asked her to have a session with me; he added on a lighter note 'take him over and console him', and then he gave me a gentle pat on the back.

The lady led my wife and me over to the same room, where I had met with her the previous week. Once again she tried her best to offer some support, but on that occasion, nothing mattered. I simply reaffirmed my stand and added 'look I am a Christian; I know the power of prayer and I am going to pray for God to heal me, I won't have another operation'. She said to me; Joseph, I appreciate your faith, but I also think the best thing to do is to let the doctors do what they can. She assured me that others have gone through the same pathway and have returned to normal life. She offered that if I would be interested, she could arrange for me to meet a lady who went through a similar procedure. Though hers was on a slightly smaller scale and with no radiotherapy; this would hopefully give me some assurances. She felt it might also help me decide after seeing someone who had gone through it and was looking normal. I said if you want to do that, it's fine with me, but I knew nothing was going to change my mind anyway.

THE FIGHT OF FAITH

I left the hospital with mixed feelings of anger and a determination to draw God's attention to this matter. That day, I was on a routine one day fast. Without seeking the consent of my wife, who was very particular about what I was taking in after the initial operation; I decided to continue the fast from that day on for a whole week. Within the week, I was determined to go for three consecutive days with no food at all. Later that evening I prayed my heart out, weeping bitterly for the first time since the whole issue came up. My prayers were based on 2Kings 16:20-19:4; particularly on chapter 19:1-3.

> *As soon as King Hezekiah heard their report, he tore his clothes in grief, put on sackcloth, and went to the Temple of the LORD. He sent Eliakim, the official in charge of the palace, Shebna, the court secretary, and the senior priests to the prophet Isaiah son of Amoz. They also were wearing sackcloth. This is the message which he told them to give Isaiah: "Today is a day of suffering; we are being punished and are in disgrace. We are like a woman who is ready to give birth, but is too weak to do it* **(2Kings 19:1-3 GNB).**

Against this background, I reminded God that He had groomed me with lots of abilities. However, at the time that I was to give birth and be of more blessing to my generation, my strength had been drained. My life was like a woman who had carried a pregnancy for nine months and when it mattered most, she did not have the strength to deliver. So the baby dies. I asked God not to allow all that He had prepared me for to go down to the grave. I had just published my first book *'The Hidden Power of Forgiveness'* that was blessing many people, and I had ideas about other books I wanted to write. I mentioned everything I thought would be wasted if God allowed me to die. I was also seeking a word from Him to confirm my decision not go ahead with the operation. I was desperately seeking God to endorse my decision before other people hear about it and confuse me by talking me into it. Up until this moment, I had only informed the senior pastor of the church and my wife; no other person had an inclination of the developments within the last week. Anyone who saw me not looking my usual self would obviously relate it to the earlier operation I had undergone not too long before then.

While I was dealing with these issues; the wound of the earlier operation developed an abscess (an infected swelling), which later burst open, oozing out significant amount of puss. Due to the antibiotics and other medication that was prescribed I could not carry on with my three days fasting without food; however, I carried on with the day to day fast for the next seven days, breaking the fast with light food every evening. My wife didn't like the idea; she felt I was in a phase of reduced immunity and needed to eat well. I thought, if only she could comprehend how I felt she wouldn't disturb me with the need to build up my immunity. During the days that followed, I informed a few other people about the state of the affairs in my life, including my friend and the senior pastor of the church in Ghana whom my son was still living with. I made him aware of my plans to take a break from any secular work to focus on my health and family and asked him to arrange to bring my boy over to me. I also contacted my research partners at the University of Nottingham and made them aware that I was giving up my role on the project.

During the period of fasting and prayers, two things happened that gave me strong assurance that no matter how things went, I was going to survive it. One afternoon, I had a dream, which I considered very significant, although I did not fully understand what it implied. I was standing at the edge of a big pool of water. I knew I had to swim through it but, I was not confident in swimming. As a result, I was prepared to walk through only as far as my feet would still be holding on to the floor of the pool. I was not prepared to go further into deeper waters, where my feet could lose its grip on the floor and I would be required to swim to stay afloat. However, at that critical point, someone pushed me with force, surging me into the deeper water, where I necessarily had to swim to survive. Surprisingly, I did not panic; my attempt to swim out of the deep water was effortless. Most importantly, I simultaneously found myself swimming freely on the surface of the water. Just then I woke up from the nap. What does this mean? I asked myself. Does it really mean God wanted me to take up some assignment, which I did not have enough faith for, and something had to push me into it to find out how easy it is to do what He wanted me to do? Or did it imply an evil hand had pushed me into deeper waters, but God was there to see me through? Whatever it meant, it was very reassuring to me. At least I could conclude that no matter how scary and deep the issues I was praying about were, I wasn't going to sink; I was going to come through it.

The second thing that gave me such strong assurance of God's presence with me was a passage from scripture. I had been given up to Wednesday, the 23rd of December to come out with my final decision. Meanwhile, I had been informed that the MDT meeting had endorsed the consultant's recommendations. Also the MRI and chest X-ray results had come through indicating the cancer had not spread anywhere else to cause serious concern. It was explained to me that if it had, it may not have been worth taking me through all that even if I decided I wanted the operation. So again on Sunday, the 20th, I decided to fulfil my commitment to go on a full three days fasting without food; perhaps God would speak to me through that. On the first day of the fast, I was listening to the reading of scriptures from the Old Testament on my MP3 prayer. In the process, I fell asleep while listening to the last chapter of the Book of Esther but woke up when the reading had gotten to Job Chapter 11: 15 and the words that followed down to the end of the chapter pierced through my heart as if God had carved out those words just in time for me.

> *'Surely then you shall lift up your face without spot; yea, you shall be steadfast and shall not fear; for you shall forget your misery, and you shall remember it as waters that pass away. And your lifetime shall be clearer than the noonday; though there be darkness, you shall be as the morning. And you shall be safe, because there is hope; yea, you shall look around you, and you shall take your rest in safety. You shall lie down, and none shall make you afraid. Yea, many shall seek your favour'* **(Job 11: 15-19 NKJV).**

I knew, this could not have been a mere coincidence; it was simply too timely and too specific to be a coincidence. For me to have woken up exactly on the verses that mattered to me was very significant. This gave me a lot of enthusiasm to carry on with my prayers. I spent lots of time alone with God. On several occasions, my wife was with me praying; by this time she had given up trying to talk me out of the series of fasting.

TIMELY INTERVENTIONS

A day before I was to go back to the senior consultant to give him my decision, I was still resolved that I wasn't going to consent the operation. I had not had a specific endorsement of my decision not to go ahead from God, I had been encouraged by the two instances I mentioned earlier that whether I did it or not, I wasn't going to die. I was going to ask them to let me go ahead with the radiotherapy.

In the course of the day, however, there were two major interventions that eventually set me thinking very hard and objectively about the possibility of going for the operation. Firstly, the lady whom the specialist nurse had arranged to meet with me could not make it and had left her contact details for me to call her, if I still wanted to hear her version. Until this day, I felt it was unnecessary to do so. But somehow, I thought it would be rude to go back the next day and inform the specialist nurse, who had gone through all that trouble to arrange the appointment that I felt it wasn't necessary. So purely out of courtesy, I decided to call up the lady. And my! Oh my!! I was pleasantly surprised to hear her speak with such clarity; there was absolutely nothing wrong with how she sounded. She explained that she had her operation a few years earlier and not too long after, she went back to work. Well, I thanked her and hanged up, ticked the box; job done! At least I had something to report back the next day. This encounter at least made me aware that it was possible to come out clean and with perfect speech, but yet I was not moved.

Meanwhile I was expecting a crucial visit from the senior pastor of my church and another leader, Pastor Olu. The senior pastor, Dr Ezekiel is a practicing GP and Pastor Olu, who is the music director of the church, is also a medical consultant, who treats breast cancers. Dr Ezekiel had heard about my decision not go ahead with the operation and had spoken to other senior pastors about it to determine the appropriate advice to give. While they were planning to visit me at home, pastor Olu requested to speak with my consultant to seek some clarifications. He wanted to do this to get a better understanding into what the procedure would entail, to guide in advising me on the way forward. Though not a Neck and Head specialist; being a consultant with expertise in cancers, he would have a better insight than me. In response to his request, I had called the secretary of the consultant, and had explained to her that a friend of mine who is a medical specialist would like to seek some clarifications over the phone from the senior consultant leading my case. She said as long as I consented, she would facilitate that. So the two consultants had spoken over the phone and Pastor Olu had gathered all the relevant information before they came to my house later that evening.

As I have indicated earlier, the senior pastor is a man of prayer and of great faith. My honest expectation, when he promised to come and see me was that he was going to back my stand and assure me of their prayer support. I had missed the point completely. I had planned to elaborate on all the prayers I had made and the assurances I had received from God, to the effect that I wasn't going to die, to buttress my decision.

To my utter disappointment, he was not ready for any spiritual jargon. He completely took me by surprise. He passionately believed that regardless of all the prayers I and they had offered he was of the strongest opinion that the operation was the right thing to do. He emphasised the fact that God has given man the wisdom to sort things out on earth and that He comes in where we are limited. But when there are clear options, we would be stupid to refuse them and claim to trust God. Pastor Olu then took over and gave me a good lecture on what he does and how people react when he explains the procedures involved to them. He then assured me that he had had a good interaction with my consultant and he is confident that everything will be fine. He added that, the people seeing me are among the best in England and that I am in very safe hands.

Pastor Ezekiel, the senior pastor, then said something that hit me like a thunderbolt. He said, Pastor Joe, who knows if it is just for this reason that God kept you in this country till now? Had it not been for the fact that you were still in the UK, we will not be here talking about your recovery; you'd most probably be dead and gone by now. That was blunt, but it did set me thinking.

I thought very deeply about that statement, and my mind scanned quickly through all the developments that had kept me in England. As I explained in an earlier chapter, God had given me a firm promise to remain in the land, and He was going to establish me and bless me. However, my personal circumstances would not have permitted it. Almost everything had worked against my continual stay in England. Then just when I was about to complete my studies and simply fly out of the country, my wife who had been looking forward to leaving, had an opportunity for further studies that made us decide for her to remain to pursue that opportunity. I also ended up becoming part of a project that tied me down to the UK to give me the opportunity to access health care. I then remembered the suffering I endured in Africa for well over seven months while working out on the fields. The hands that I was arrogantly refusing to touch me, were the same hands God used to relieve me of the excruciating pain I had endured during those months.

Before they left, they assured me that the seven-member Pastoral Executive Committee, of which I was a part, had declared three days of fasting to pray with me, and they had started that same day. That day was the last day of my three days fast without food. They had arranged a prayer meeting later that evening solely for me; they invited my wife and me to join if we could.

I was very much touched by this visit. After they had left, I began for the first time to consider the possibility of consenting to what the consultant had explained to me. This was a very challenging turning point. Following that visit I had a brief conversation with my wife, who was very relieved at the turn of events. Before joining the prayer session that evening, I had another hard look at the whole situation. And I was reminded of something that happened many years ago regarding my belief in divine healing.

I became a truly born again Christian at the tender age of 14 years. I progressed fairly smoothly through the Christian faith until my sixth form days, when I came in contact with a group of young believers who were on fire for the Lord. The group was known as Jesus to the Rural World. It was led by a group of young men and women, who had practically given up everything to bring the gospel to the most remote of places in Ghana and beyond. Everything about them was radical. During their conferences, which were dubbed variously as 'Fire Conference' or 'Spiritual Cadet Training'; we were made to pray for hours unending. We were taught to trust God for almost everything, including finances, food, healing etc. They did not believe that a person of faith should be sick in the first place; therefore medication was largely considered as a channel of healing for the faithless. In reality, to a large extent, those who believed and put these teachings into practice, these principles worked for them. On one occasion, we had ended a conference and had been sent out to a remote village to share the word of God with the indigenous people. We had no protection against mosquitoes. After less than a week of being in the village, I had a terrible bout of malaria. Practically, there was very little chance of accessing medical care even if I wanted to. But being with a group of faith-studded young Christians, I seemed to have no choice than to pray to God and trust Him for divine healing. I prayed my heart out. Miraculously, the very next day, I woke up with no trace of malaria symptoms. You can imagine the surge of faith I experienced from then on. I was beside myself with excitement for experiencing faith healing for the first time in my life. I said to myself; from that day, I was never going to have anything to do with medication ever again in my entire lifetime.

However, on another occasion, while on campus during my undergraduate days later that same year; I had another episode of malaria attack, and I was ready to go down the same lane. However, this time around, even though I did all that I did when we were out in the village, the symptoms only got worse. You will not believe what I am about to reveal; I was so determined to experience divine healing that, for a period of six months, I battled with the disease and refused to take any medicine. It was only when I could not study for my first semester examination and ended up with terrible results that I began to think again. By the time I went to the hospital, I could not tell the truth. The symptoms could not be relieved even with the strongest malaria drugs at the time. I guess the parasites had become extremely resistant. I can't tell why I lived through it. I could easily have died. It took repeated doses to slowly relieve the symptoms.

Now, the reason I remembered this situation was this: I had learnt from that experience that, when we find ourselves in situations where we run out of options, but are able to trust God to come to our aid; He will come through for us. On the other hand, when God has provided help and we refuse to access that opportunity, we may not succeed in twisting the hands of God to do our bidding. That evening, this experience rolled back to me. I wondered if it wasn't for moments such as the one I was confronted with, that God taught me that lesson early in my faith walk. Yet, I almost lost it again.

My wife and I later that evening joined the leaders to pray and I came back home with peace all over me. I broke my three days dry fast that night at about 10.00 pm and continued fasting daily for the next two days just to be part of the leaders prayer sessions organised just for me.

One important lesson I wish to bring out from this long narrative is that, in your most vulnerable moments, the people around you matter a lot in determining the direction of your life. In my case though, I believe it is the Lord who planted me in the right family to lead me to the destination where He had intended for me. I am very much grateful to God and to all the people He planted around me to help me through this challenging face of my life.

So on Wednesday, the 23rd of December, I met up with another friend of mine, who was also a consultant in tissue viability, working in the same hospital and who had offered to accompany me to meet with my consultant. He also asked all the relevant questions and assured me there was no cause for alarm. When we met up with the consultant, he asked if I had given it a thought; I said yes, I am happy for you to go ahead, please! He smiled and said 'I am happy you have made the right decision'. He added, 'if you had come back telling me you wouldn't do it, I would not be offended, but I would have been disappointed in you'. Furthermore, he said 'yes I appreciate that you believe in God; I also do, but I believe God uses the hands of men to accomplish what He wants to do'.

With the green light given, he hinted that the 'big operation' was likely to be done on the 18th of January, 2010. But before then, the procedure to insert the feeding tube would have been done and assessed to ensure that the tube was functioning properly before the main surgery date was due.

CHAPTER 4

MY IN-BETWEEN PERIOD

"Let us hold unswervingly to the hope we profess, for he who promised is faithful ....
So do not throw away your confidence, it will be richly rewarded."
(Heb 10: 23, 35 NIV).

Dear reader, from what I have narrated of my experiences so far, I wish to share some important thoughts with you before I carry on with what happened next.

There will be moments in your life as a believer when you may wonder if God is still there for you. Note that I did not say, there *may* be; I said there *will* be such moments. That is one of the reasons why I decided to write this book. My desire was to remind the reader that even when nothing seems to be happening in response to your prayers, God has promised never to leave us nor forsake us; He will still be at work on what you pray to Him for.

During a very difficult moment in my life, when I could not feel God's presence in any way, someone forwarded to me an e-mail message with two remarkable statements. Those statements brought me great motivation, which gave me the strength to move on. It stated that every true believer should be reminded that *"when you are down to nothing, God is up to something"*. The second statement also assured that *"if God has brought you to it, he will see you through it"*. I took those statements as messages from heaven to me, because I was at a moment in my life where I was asking if God had indeed been involved in my case from the beginning. Today, I can say with no shadow of doubt that He had always been there.

Has God said anything concerning you, which appears to have fallen through? Or are you experiencing delays in the fulfilment of a promise of God that makes you wonder whether it was God you heard in the first place? Take this exhortation from me that the most difficult period when waiting for the fulfilment of a promise of God is what I refer to as the *"In-Between"* period. When God asked Abraham to leave his people and go to a land He would show him (Gen 12:1-3), He only gave him instruction concerning the beginning of the faith journey and the promise at the end of the journey. He said to Abraham *'leave and I will bless you'*. God did not mention anything about the challenges of the *In-Between* period. Have you ever reflected on the issues Abraham had to contend with before the promised end came? God is referred to as the Alpha and the Omega or the Beginning and the End; but don't ever forget that he is also the God of the *In-Between* period. Is there silence in your life concerning a promise, which you may have been trusting God for? It does not necessarily mean God is not at work; if he did speak, then *He must be up to something.*

In scripture, the account of how God chose the first king of Israel has served as a motivation to me in many situations in my life. I do not give up on life or any endeavour of faith simply because of what may be happening in the present.

When Saul's family lost their donkeys and he was chosen to go and look for them with one of the servants, it could not have been a pleasurable errand (1Sam 9). After travelling through the thickets of the wilderness for a number of days without finding the donkeys, he became so frustrated that he wanted to give up and return home. It took only the intervention of the servant he was moving around with, to decide to go ahead. The beauty of the story, however, is that about the time he was considering giving up the search and return home, God was busy instructing Samuel that by the next day, Saul was to be enthroned as the first king of Israel. God said *"About this time tomorrow,* **I will send you a man** *from the land of Benjamin. Anoint him leader over my people Israel".* Isn't it amazing that the errand and its related challenges were not about the missing donkeys? *God was up to something* far greater and of much more importance than the missing donkeys. It was about the fulfilment of a destiny, which Saul himself could not have imagined. And does it not surprise you why God did not simply reveal to him what he was up to or why he chose such an unusual pathway to fulfil his intentions concerning Saul? Yea, He is God; He does not owe us any explanation of how He does His things. That is another reason why it is essential to trust God to the end after we have committed an issue to Him: *'Commit thy way unto the LORD; trust also in him; and he shall bring it to pass* **(Psalms 37:5 KJV)**. At the peak of Saul's frustration, God was also at the peak of His action concerning him; but he simply did not know what God was up to. His ways are not your ways, neither are His thoughts your thoughts.

Sadly, many of us so easily give up and turn our backs to God when the going gets tough; particularly when we seem not to comprehend what God is up to. If you are contemplating giving up on any faith endeavour, may I declare to you that you have come too far to miss out:

> *"Let us hold unswervingly to the hope we profess, for he who promised is faithful . . . . So do not throw away your confidence, it will be richly rewarded. You need to persevere so that when you have done the will of God, you will receive what he has promised. For in just a very little while, he who is coming will come and will not delay. But my righteous one will live by faith. And if he shrinks back, I will not be pleased with him"* **(Heb 10: 23, 35-38 NIV).**

While reading through the Book of Habakkuk, my interest was aroused when I noted that although the prophet was facing apparent difficulties, he remained joyful and steadfast in faith. I wondered how his faith could remain resolute in the face of the challenging situation he was confronted with. The concluding verses of the book of Habakkuk read:

> **(Habakkuk 3:17-19 NIV)** *"Though the fig tree does not bud, and there are no grapes on the vines, though the olive crop fails and the fields produce no food, though there are no sheep in the pen and no cattle in the stalls, Yet I will rejoice in the LORD, I will be joyful in God my Saviour. The Sovereign LORD is my strength; he makes my feet like the feet of a deer, he enables me to go on the heights".*

While I sought to understand the reason for this strength in the face of lack, I found the answer in an earlier chapter. The Prophet Habakkuk had complained to God about the injustices and violence of his generation. In response, God had given him a word about how he would deal with the situation to allow righteousness to prevail again. The LORD however told him to mark it carefully. God said to Him *"The revelation awaits an appointed time;—and will not prove false, Though it linger, wait for it; it will certainly come and will not delay"* **(Habakkuk 2:3).** There are some important lessons here for us to take note of.

Firstly, God has His own timing concerning His promises; which is *"God's appointed time".* When the appointed time concerning a divine promise is due, there is no delay at all in its fulfilment. Indeed in His time, He makes all things beautiful. The expression *"Though it linger"* reveals a different timing; our own expectations or our *"expected time".* It is only in relation to our own timing that a promise of God could linger or delay. Once God has given a word, he expects us to hang onto it unswervingly, for *"the just shall live by faith"* **(Habakkuk 2:4b KJV).** The prophet surely understood this, for which reason he could go through the persistent difficulties of the *"now",* and still remain resolute in faith; knowing that it was just a matter of time for the promise to be fulfilled.

If God has given you a word about any issue in your life then please do not focus on any contrary circumstances that you may be experiencing. Simply hold on to His word and keep trusting Him. In His time He will make all things beautiful.

The Lord had clearly spoken to me, but for many years, things did not seem to be in place for me to experience what God had said to me. By this stage, the challenging developments in my life, which had completely overshadowed everything God had originally said to me; could be related quite closely with one of my favourite stories in the Old Testament. The future God revealed to Joseph through his dreams and the long delays he experienced before he was vindicated to fulfil those dreams, have so much for us to learn from. If you ever take time out to read this account from the book of Genesis chapters 37 all the way through chapter 50, you will most likely wonder at some point what God was up to during those lengthy and consistently difficult years in the life of this faithful young man. Amazingly, however, though Joseph couldn't understand what had become of the great promises God had given him through his dreams, that he would be a great man; he neither gave up nor rebelled against God. During those depressing periods of his life, he did not let go of his values. When Potiphar's wife tried to lure him to come into her bed, it was the fear or reverence he still had for God that prevented him from doing so; he said *"I cannot do this and sin against my God"*, yes the same God who had allowed him to be sold into slavery. The truth is this; as long as a child of God remains faithful to God, everything works out for good. Even what was meant for evil, God could turn it around for good. Joseph did not shrink back, and God was pleased with him. *"For the eyes of the LORD range throughout the earth to strengthen those whose hearts are fully committed to him"* (2Chron 16:9a NIV). Joseph's commitment to remain faithful to God even landed him in prison after Potiphar's wife accused him of attempted rape. Yet he did not give up his faith in God.

Unknown to Joseph, God was preparing him for an assignment that would save not only his life, but his entire family and the whole region from death and destruction. When God's time was ripe, it took just a day to bring him out of prison to become the second most important person in Egypt; the land into which he was sold as a slave.

Having been involved in a scheme to store up enough food in the seven years preceding the most devastating hunger to hit the region, Joseph had been made the top man in charge of food stores. Most likely, after such long spell of difficulties, Joseph must have forgotten what God had told him over 20 years earlier while still a teenager. But God had prepared the stage to remind him of what He had determined to do with his life. The emphasised portion of the passage below was what triggered his memory to remember vividly what God had said to him many years earlier:

> *When Jacob learned that there was grain in Egypt, he said to his sons, "Why do you just keep looking at each other?" He continued, "I have heard that there is grain in Egypt. Go down there and buy some for us, so that we may live and not die." Then ten of Joseph's brothers went down to buy grain from Egypt—So Israel's sons were among those who went to buy grain, for the famine was in the land of Canaan also. Now Joseph was the governor of the land, the one who sold grain to all its people.* **So when Joseph's brothers arrived, they bowed down to him with their faces to the ground.** *As soon as Joseph saw his brothers, he recognized them—Although Joseph recognized his brothers, they did not recognize him.* **Then he remembered his dreams about them**—(Gen 42:1-9).

On that fateful day, as his brothers bowed before him, Joseph remembered what the Lord had told him over two decade earlier in his dreams. God had spoken from the *'beginning'*; He had showed him the *'end'*, but He gave no indication of what was to happen in the *'in-between'* before the end would come.

May I declare to you dear reader, that if only you will remain faithful to God; in due course, as the Lord unfolds his plans for your life, you will surely remember everything he has said concerning you. None of them will fail. It will not matter who intends to keep you down; they can only do so for as long as the Lord allows them. But when his appointed time is due, the promised elevation will come in ways you could not have imagined. You only need to ensure that you remain pleasing to the Lord. In the history of Israel, there was a time when the prevailing challenges they were confronted with made them conclude that there was no way the promises of God concerning them could come to pass. On that occasion, Joshua said to them

> *"If the LORD is pleased with us, he will lead us into that land, a land flowing with milk and honey, and will give it to us. Only do not rebel against the LORD. And do not be afraid of the people of the land, because we will swallow them up. Their protection is gone, but the LORD is with us. Do not be afraid of them."* **(Num 14: 8-9)**.

These thoughts and the manner in which God kept showing up through revelations, as well as the people he brought my way, served as crucial motivational factors to look into the future with hope. Regardless of the uncertainties staring me in the face, I had the courage to look forward to a wonderful future of fulfilled life.

CHAPTER 5

TREATMENTS AND HELP FROM ABOVE

I will lift up mine eyes unto the hills, from whence cometh my help. My help cometh from the LORD, which made heaven and earth
(Psalm 121:1-2)

On Thursday, the 14th of January 2010, I reported for the second time to the Ear Nose and Throat (ENT) ward C-24 of the Queen's Medical Centre (QMC), where I was prepared for a Gastrostomy (PEG) tube to be inserted in my tummy. I was moved to another unit within the hospital complex for this minor surgical procedure.

THE INSERTION OF PEG

PEG is the short form or initials for Percutaneous Endoscopic Gastrostomy; it is a procedure that allows a specialist—an endoscopist—to look into the stomach and the first part of the bowel of the patient to guide in inserting a feeding tube in the stomach. Clark *et al* (2006) explain some of the activities during the procedure:

- Most people will have the back of their throat sprayed with a local anaesthetic spray and a sedative given intravenously.

- A flexible endoscopy tube is passed over the back of your tongue, down your gullet, into your stomach and the first part of your small bowel.

- Air is put into your stomach so that a clear view of the lining of your stomach can be seen. This may cause you to feel bloated during and after the procedure.

- Light from the end of the flexible endoscopy tube will be seen from within the stomach to the surface of the skin. A second Endoscopist presses on this area with a finger to check the correct position for the feeding tube.

- A local anaesthetic is injected at the chosen site to numb the area. A small cut is then made into the numbed area and a needle is passed through into the stomach.

- The flexible endoscopy tube is then taken out and the feeding tube is then passed through the mouth, into the stomach and then out through the small cut in your abdominal wall and secured to the wall of the stomach.

Though Clark *et al* (2006) do not mention the inclusion of a camera in the procedure, while under sedation, I suppose the thin tube passed through my throat into my stomach had a tiny camera attached to the tip; I was somehow conscious and could see the internal tissues of my stomach on a screen, which guided the endoscopist in the procedure.

CHAPTER 5 - TREATMENTS AND HELP FROM ABOVE

By the time I had fully recovered from the effects of the sedation, I found a tube sticking out of my belly wall (see Pictures in plate 2). I had been laid on a stretcher and wheeled back to C-24, where I stayed overnight. I was not permitted any food. After several hours, a nurse came to set up a pump to allow water to run through the feeding tube for the first time. The pump was set to run for eight hours. By the next day, I was very hungry; I had not had any food for over 24 hours but I was not yet permitted to eat. It was essential to ensure that there were no complications with the tube.

Plate 2

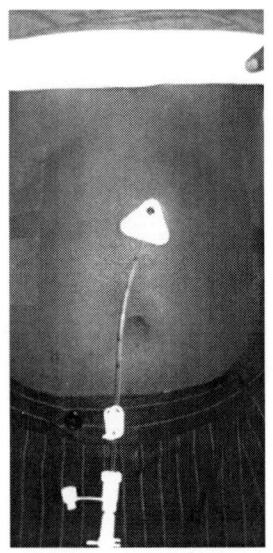
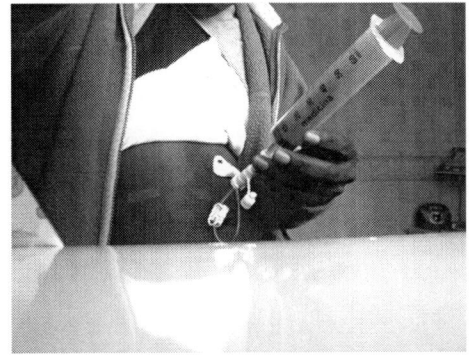

(a) *PEG Feeding Tube*   (b) *Flushing down water with a syringe through the PEG tube*

Later that day, the 15th of January 2010, I was discharged with permission to eat through my mouth but with a caution to be careful not to overdo it. The site of insertion was now quite sore as the anaesthesia had worn out. As explained earlier, the PEG tube was needed because I was not going to be able to feed or drink through my mouth after the big operation, which was due in a few days. The tube indeed proved to be extremely useful, particularly during the peak of the radiotherapy treatment.

THE 'BIG OPERATION'

On Sunday the 17th of Jan 2010, after returning from church service, I went back to the ward C-24 at the QMC for the third time. The first admission was to remove the lump and the second for the insertion of the PEG feeding tube. On this occasion, it was for the 'big operation' as the medical team referred to it. The procedure was scheduled for the next morning.

I was very confident that I had taken the right decision and that God was fully in control. I was not too nervous as in the case of the first operation. As mentioned earlier, the first operation was my first time to be admitted to a hospital in my entire lifetime. I was nervous, not for being admitted to a hospital; it was the thought that I was about to undergo an operation which was such a big deal to me then. This time however, I was very calm. All the routine observations, including my pulse rate, were normal. That evening, I was visited by one of the registrars of the Maxillofacial Unit, who explained in detail all the procedures that were to be performed on me. It was that night that I learnt for the first time, that most of the top and lower teeth on the left side of my mouth, where the procedure was to be performed, will need to be removed for the specialists to have easy access to perform the procedure. I listened carefully, and then I signed the consent form handed out to me. By doing so, I had given the medical team my permission to do whatever they deemed right after putting me to sleep under general anaesthesia. The implications were huge; having signed the consent form, I would have no grounds to complain about anything they did to achieve their objective of giving me a chance to live. I did have a pretty normal sleep that night without any apprehension.

The next morning, Monday, the 18th of January, 2010, I was wheeled to a room next to the theatre at about 7.30 am, where I met the Anaesthetist. She was the same person who handled my first operation. She was very pleasant and tried to let me feel relaxed. It was around 8.00 am when she finally asked if it was alright with me for her to put me to sleep. I nodded to signify my consent; that was it . . . .

I regained consciousness at about 10.00 pm that same day and was told I was in a recovery ward with a nurse assigned to me. By the time I fully recovered from the effects of the anaesthesia, I noted that I could not speak. There were several tubes sticking out from different parts of my body and connected to different gadgets and monitors. They included a drain, sticking out of the operation site, a catheter, oxygen pump, Patient Controlled Analgesia (PCA) machine for morphine, drips going through my feet and the back of my right wrist and my left arm was in a cast (POP) from my wrist up to the elbow, various monitors etc. I could hardly move any part of my body. The Consultant later came over and told me that it all went very well. He added that he had spoken to my wife over the phone a couple of hours earlier and had assured her everything went well. After an intensive period of care, I was wheeled on the stretcher carefully to the High Dependency Unit (HDU) with most of the gadgets intact.

I later learnt that the operation took up to 12 hours. My wife later explained to me that she made frantic efforts to speak to someone during the day about the progress, but there was no one available. It was after 7.00 pm that she received a call from the Consultant assuring her that the worst was over and that the other members of the team were closing up the wounds. When the surgeon came to see me in the recovery area, he explained that he began the operation with a team of doctors and carried on for about 6 hours before he handed over to the second surgeon in the unit to finish off with other team of doctors. In total, I was told a sizable team, comprising two consultants, a number of registrars, senior house officers, young doctors and students were involved in the operation.

I understood that in the process, a cut had been made into my wind pipe, through the lower part of my neck; a process which is referred to as tracheostomy. A plastic tube-set, known as a tracheostomy tube was then inserted into the wind pipe and sutured to the skin on my neck to secure it in place to facilitate breathing after the operation. Having secured that in place, the earlier operation site was then opened up again and widened further. I learnt that subsequently, a number of glands, lymph nodes, surrounding tissues, teeth, part of the lining of the mouth and so on were then removed. The concept was that tissues and organs close to the area where the lump had been located, and which the consultant felt could potentially be affected by malignant cells, were simply taken out to reduce the chances of recurrence.

Following the removal of the tissues, the area affected was then reconstructed with a piece of skin and vein, which had been taken from my left forearm. They referred to the reconstructed part under the left side of my tongue as the flap. My understanding was that the vein from my arm was connected to another vein in the neck area to continue to supply blood to the flap; else the cells would die pretty quickly. From my left arm, a piece of skin had then been taken from the upper part of the forearm to close up the area where the flap was taken and the whole area was then sutured up. That was the reason my left arm was in a cast.

At the HDU, some of the gadgets, which had been disconnected to allow me to be wheeled from the recovery area, were reconnected. A nurse came over and introduced herself as the one who will be staying dedicatedly with me throughout the night. She assured me that there were standard gadgets and screens to monitor every development and that she was going to be by me all the way through. That was reassuring, because I was wondering how I could make them aware if anything went wrong with me; remember I could not speak and I could hardly move.

While I lay quietly on the bed, which had been adjusted to allow my head and the upper part of my body to be slightly raised, I could see three other patients with similar gadgets and individual nurses taking care of them. Some could talk and explain what they wanted to say to their nurses. Gradually, the realisation dawned on me that I wasn't going to be able to talk to anyone for a while; I felt tightness in my throat and remembered then that a tracheostomy tube had been inserted, through which I was now breathing. I had been made aware that I would be given a jotter to write out whatever I would want to communicate, but that was to come much later, as the gadgets in place would not permit any such movement at the time. I also remembered the PEG feeding tube and the fact that I wasn't going to be able to eat through my mouth for a while.

While I was still contemplating the full implications of what I had just been through, a senior house officer (a young lady doctor) who had come to see me earlier in the recovery ward came back to me and explained that they will need to be checking on the flap in my mouth every hour for the next 48 hours, to be sure nothing goes wrong. She explained that the first 48 hours was crucial in determining whether the flap was successful or not. Within that time frame, it was vital to pick up any anomaly on the flap within an hour, to have a good chance of being able to rectify it. Otherwise there could be unimaginable implications that could involve going back to the theatre. As a result, I had to literally stay awake for the next two days, with no sleep at all. I could only dose off for a short time before the next checking was due. The doctor would place a gadget on the flap and listen for the pulsating sound that signified that blood was running through the skin, which was now lining the left side of the lower floor of my mouth. It was exciting to see the elation on the faces of the doctors whenever the gadget was placed on the flap and we both heard the sounds *'puhf-puhf-puhf-puhf-puhf . . . !'* Additionally, they would also feel the flap with the hand to be sure it was warm enough. Those two observations implied the flap was very much alive. Though it was very difficult going without sleep after such a major procedure, the joy of learning hour after hour that the delicately reconstructed flap was doing the job the doctors expected, was gratifying.

There were, however some moments of concern during the first few hours following the surgery. On two occasions during the first night, I felt very sick and threw up. The nurse taking care of me was very helpful; I also had a suction, which I used regularly to clear my mouth of fluids, since I could not swallow. On another occasion, the tracheostomy tubes were getting clogged up making me struggle to breath. When the nurse attempted to replace the inner piece of the tracheostomy tube, it felt very irritating and I was forced to cough repeatedly. It felt very weird to realise that the phlegm were gushing out from my neck rather than my mouth or nose.

That night, obviously was indeed a very long one. As I reclined in my bed, unable to sleep or move, I reflected deeply. Suddenly, the immense value and privilege of being able to wake up each morning and simply jump out of bed to do whatever I wanted became so real to me. I was overwhelmed with a deep desire to thank God for the little things of life, but I could only do so in my mind and heart. Oh! If only we could appreciate the 'little things' we take for granted in everyday life, we will have a lot to thank and praise God for. I wish to encourage you, dear reader to stop and consider what you can do and simply thank God for them; there is indeed a lot to thank Him for in our lives.

MIRACULOUS RECOVERY

The next morning, Tuesday, the 19th, a team of about 15 medical staff; including the lead surgeon, registrars, senior house officers, house officers, and students came over to the HDU to see me. They were very pleased at my progress of recovery. I learnt that usually, many patients who undergo this type and extent of surgery would have a swollen neck and face by the next day; they remarked that I didn't look different from my normal self. The original plan was for me to spend 48 hours in HDU, but following the observations of the team that morning, the plan was immediately changed. An instruction was given for me to be moved from high dependency to the main ward. They advised the care team to sit me up, get a physiotherapist to try and get me to stand and if all went well, I should then be transferred to the ward. A male nurse and a lady student had now taken over from the night nurse in taking care of me. They gave me a bath in bed, sat me down and got me ready to be wheeled to the main wards. A pastor friend, who also worked as a consultant in the hospital was the only relation, who due to his position, was able to have access to see me in the HDU. Even my wife was not given access to see me.

That afternoon at about 12 noon, i.e. less than 24 hours after the big operation, I was transferred with all the tubes still in place to a single occupancy room (side room) in the ENT ward, C-24. I laid in bed the whole time till the next morning. It was this day that my wife was able to see me for the first time after the operation. I was with mixed feelings to see her. We were both grateful to God that the worst was over, but my inability to speak to her was hard to take. I had then been given a jotter to write out what I wanted to say. We couldn't communicate much; we were just happy to be together. That was when the pictures below were taken (see pictures in plate 3)

The hourly observation of the flap continued throughout the whole day and night. As the doctors and nurses walk into the room, I could see the delight on their faces as they saw me meet them with a smile. A nurse remarked *'wow! Joseph, you don't look different; by now most people would be swollen'*. The most common comment I heard from the medical staff, when they walked into the side room was *'you are doing so well'*.

Plate 3: A few days after the 'Big Operation'

Plate 3a

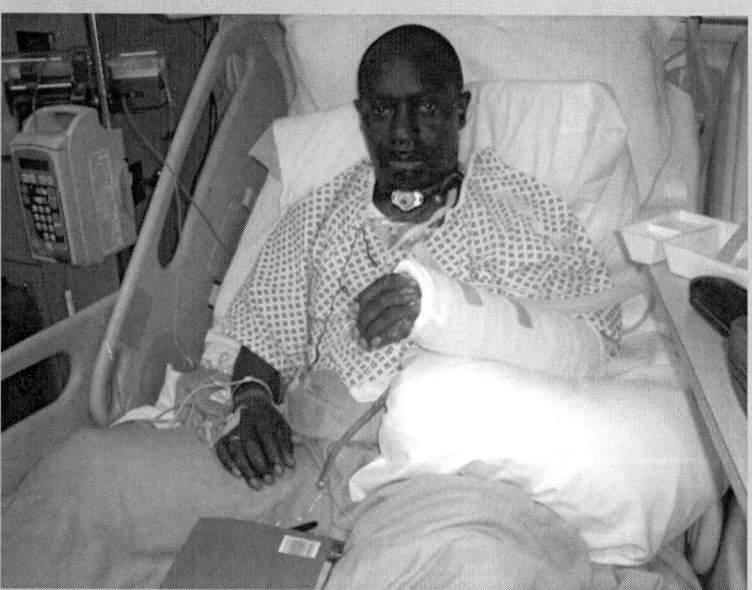

Plate 3b

CHAPTER 5 - TREATMENTS AND HELP FROM ABOVE

On the third day after the operation, on Wednesday the 20th, the catheter was allowed to be taken out, as well as all the tubes, infusions and the drain. The only supporting gadgets left on me were the oxygen and of course the PEG, which was now the only means through which my nutritional needs were being met. The PCA machine, which I was to press from time to time to release morphine directly into my veins to relieve the pain, had to be taken off; to the amazement of the medical team, I hardly used it. The few times I used it, I was prompted by the medical staff to do so. I honestly did not need it; I was not in that much pain to resort to morphine.

With the tubes off, I felt so free and in control. I was able to sit up for most part of the day. Once again I recognised the value of having the ability to walk about without much restriction. I was so grateful to God for being so good to me in bringing me this far. That was a very lively day because other visitors were permitted to come and see me. The senior pastor of my church and several of the leaders and members trooped in at various times; it was extremely encouraging. I spent the time between the visits listening to songs and reading the word of God.

On Thursday the 21st, I had a little more sleep as the flap observations went from 1 hourly to 2 hourly. The doctors came on their usual rounds in the morning and were obviously pleased. Most significantly, they requested for the inner tube of the tracheostomy to be replaced with a type that could permit me to speak if I wanted to; all I needed to do was to cover the tip with my hand to permit air to go over my voice box to make speaking possible. The change was made instantly and my first words in four days were 'good morning everyone'. There was real excitement among the medical team. I also was able to go to the bathroom and gave myself a shower and a reasonable clean up. I Praised God for how good He had been to me.

Following the apparent rapid progress I made in recovery, the decision was taken for my children to come and see me. As at that stage, they did not know that I had been battling with cancer, but they had been prepared for what to expect on their visit. It was during the visit that I explained briefly why I needed to go through all that. They had many questions but, as I was struggling to speak, we agreed to discuss in detail and answer all their questions after I had been discharged.

The day continued to be a very happy one; several leaders and members of the church, friends and colleagues trooped in to see me. Later that evening, I was able to walk out of my room into the public areas for the first time and the nurses and other medical staff were pleased at the progress I had made; though I wasn't sure at this stage, how different my recovery was in comparison with others who had been through the similar magnitude of the operation. While seeing off a couple who had come to see me, one of the nurses who last saw me when I was being stretchered back to the ward from the HDU, saw me from a distance and shouted 'wooooooooowww! Wow!! Is this you?' She literally run towards me and gave me a big hug, beaming with smiles. The friend I was seeing off turned to me and said, 'Pastor Joe, you have become a celebrity in this ward'.

The checks on the flap gradually became less frequent, giving me the opportunity to enjoy some hours of sleep before being interrupted. I only stayed in bed when I wanted to sleep. That night I spent some time in quite meditation. I concluded that, as scripture says *'this undoubtedly was the Lord's doing, and it was marvellous in my eyes'* **(Matt 21:42b)**.

The marvellous hand of God in my recovery process became even more apparent the next day, Friday the 22nd when the doctors came on their usual rounds. I had earlier been told during the pre-operation consultation that the tracheostomy tube could be in place for two weeks. That morning, during the doctors' rounds, which was led by the lead surgeon, he remarked that he was quite certain that I could do without the tracheostomy and therefore advised that the tube should be completely removed. That afternoon, around 3.50 pm, one of the doctors came over and following standard protocol, took out the whole piece in a fairly straightforward procedure. The wound was dressed to be sutured up the next day. What great relief that was! After the procedure, the doctor remarked 'I wish every one of our patients was as straightforward as you'.

With the dressing over the wound, I could now speak without the need to cover the cut in my neck. From then on, the clarity of my speech became another surprising observation to the medical team. I'm not sure how they interpreted it, but I knew without a shadow of doubt, that the God I serve had raised His mighty hand over me. Not only had the anticipated two weeks of discomfort been scaled down to just four days, but most importantly, any fears about possible effects on my ability to speak legibly after the operation, was quickly dispersed. You will recall that this was one of the major reasons I initially refused to submit to the procedure. Being able to speak clearly meant so much to me; how great is our God!

On the next day, Saturday the 23rd, the tracheostomy wound was stitched up by a young lady doctor. She confirmed to me that so far, the medical team considered my recovery as being their best outcome of all the patients who had gone through similar magnitude of operation. Later, the consultant came to see me and met me with a visiting friend. He commented about the clarity of my speech and cautioned me to slow down. He referred to a situation in the past when a patient pulled a stitch while trying to talk not too long after the procedure.

On Sunday, the 24th, I took a proper shower for the first time after the operation. I also had the opportunity to visit the hospital chapel to partake in a service conducted by the Church of England. I was later visited by the consultant, who to my pleasant amazement gave me the go ahead to start taking water by mouth, but to do it slowly. The next morning, Monday the 25th, the doctors' rounds involved about 15 personnel. The team was obviously happy with the progress of my recovery; consequently, the consultant confirmed that I should be discharged. In effect, the anticipated two week minimum stay in the hospital was reduced to one week. By 1.00 pm that afternoon, I arrived home to meet my family, who were eagerly waiting for me.

The final series of events in the developments that gave me clear conviction that my recovery had been a miracle orchestrated by God, occurred during my first visit to the outpatients' clinic two days after my discharge from the hospital. When I got to the clinic, a number of the nurses who had been part of the team that prepared me for the major operation were visibly elated. Before the first operation, I had lost weight from 75 kg, which was my normal body weight to 64 kg. When my body weight was checked on that occasion, it had gone up to 67 kg. I was then called to the consulting room to see one of the registrars who was to review my progress.

There were a number of personnel in the consulting room. As soon as I entered and greeted the team, the registrar who was to review my progress exclaimed **'your speech is good'**. She then went ahead and removed the cast from my left arm. I saw for the first time the section where the flap was taken from. Again the registrar remarked with amazement that the wound was healing very rapidly. The dialogue that ensued from then on finally settled the matter in my heart that indeed, it had been the doing of the Lord. In trying to explain the rate of my recovery, one of the members of the team—the doctor who had earlier removed the tracheostomy and remarked that they wished all their patients were as straightforward like me—said to me **'you have good skin or perhaps it's your genes; you have good genes'**. By then the consultant was said to be in a meeting. Soon afterwards, when they learnt he had finished with the meeting and had come to the clinic, the nurse attending to me wanted him to see me. I heard her shout out 'yes, it's good you're here; please come, Joseph is here'. When he came in and saw me, he did not make any comment; he simply smiled and stood quietly observing what was going on. I then turned to him and asked, 'sir, when can I start driving?' He laughed; then with a very calm tone, he said "**Joseph, you are doing very well. I know you got help from UP THERE, but well done.**"

That afternoon, when in answer to another enquiry, the consultant repeated that expression 'you got help from up there' referring to God's intervention; the reality of what God had done for me once again struck me. That remark from the consultant confirmed to me that the entire medical team indeed admitted that my recovery was out of the ordinary. Some attributed it to my determination to stay above the situation, others attributed it to good skin or good genes, but I knew God had established a clear difference between my case and any other they had experienced. I was happy that I had made them aware of my reasons for initially refusing to consent for the big operation. I had explained to some members of the team that I was a preacher, and rather than risking losing my vital organs for ministry, I would rather believe God to heal me. This was what prompted the consultant to acknowledge that he knew I had help from up there. If these series of occurrences did not signify divine intervention, then I don't know what else could have resulted in such an unusual sequence of outcomes in a single case. This undoubtedly, was the doing of the Lord!

THE RADIOTHERAPY TREATMENT

These experiences had so lifted my spirits that the concerns surrounding the whole experience had turned to pure joy. I had very little idea of what was to follow. I had been made aware from the start of the treatment that, due to the aggressive nature of the high grade cancer cells they detected, I will need to undergo radiotherapy treatment. Although the big surgical operation was intended to remove every tissue that could potentially be affected by cancer, the radiotherapy treatment was to further ensure that any affected cell or tissue not visible to the naked eye was destroyed.

WHAT IS RADIOTHERAPY?

Macmillan Cancer Support summarises what the treatment involves on its website *www.macmillan.org.uk.* It involves the use of high-energy rays, usually x-rays to destroy the cancer cells in the area being treated. The challenge associated with the treatment is that normal cells in the area being treated can also be damaged, although they can usually repair themselves, whereas cancer cells cannot.

There are two ways of giving radiotherapy: external beam radiotherapy (also known as external radiotherapy) and internal radiotherapy. It was recommended for me to undergo external radiotherapy, which is given from outside the body using high-energy x-rays.

The treatment involves having a course of treatments given once a day from Monday to Friday, lasting for two to seven weeks. Each treatment is called a fraction. Giving the treatment in fractions makes sure that less damage is done to normal cells than to cancer cells. Usually, each radiotherapy appointment takes about 10-30 minutes. The radiographers position the patient on the treatment couch and place a specially prepared mask over the area to be treated for stability. Once in the correct position, the radiographers leave the room before the treatment is administered. During the treatment, they are able to watch the patient from the next room to intervene if necessary.

Once the treatment session has finished, the radiographers will come back into the room and will help the patient off the treatment couch.

TREATMENT AND SIDE EFFECTS:

I was scheduled to undergo six and a half weeks of the treatment; a period I usually refer to as the most gruesome experience I've ever endured in my life. The treatment commenced on February 25th 2010 and within a week, I began experiencing uncomfortable side effects. The medical team had taken time to explain all the possible side effects, but I was completely unprepared for what I endured during those weeks. Three weeks into the treatment, my throat had become very sore. Swallowing was so difficult that I had stopped eating by mouth. That was when I fully appreciated the value of the PEC feeding tube, which had earlier been inserted through my tummy into my stomach. That was my main channel for meeting my nutritional needs for several weeks. Besides, the skin of the area had been darkening gradually, and by this stage it had distinctively turned very dark and sore.

By Friday the 26th of March, I wanted to give up on the treatment; I felt I couldn't endure the pain and 'torture' anymore. I was suffering from severe dry mouth; it was as if my salivary glands had all been destroyed. To make matters worse, thick flow of sputum, some phloem-like substance clogged my throat. Attempts to cough it out bruised the throat, which at this stage was very sore. Fresh blood stained the sputum, gushing out every time I attempted to clear my throat. It was the toughest phase of the entire experience. I could not sleep well; most times I sat up in the sofa all night and kept away from the rest of the family. Life was really challenging for the entire family. I was given some medication to relieve the pain but they did not help much. A few days later, parts of the darkened skin in the treated area began to peel off, leaving fresh sores all around my neck (see pictures in plate 4).

I did not give up; I went through till the end. To my great relief, on the 12th of April, 2010, I endured the final fraction of the radiotherapy treatment.

Plate 4:

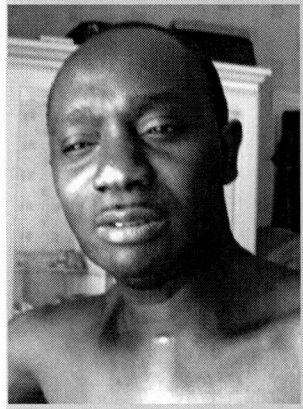 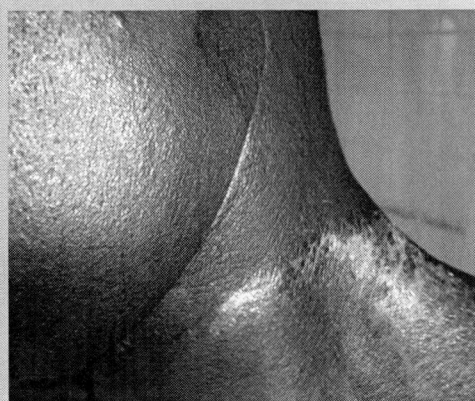

Plate 4a: Midway Through Radiotherapy Treatment

Plate 4b: Towards the end of Radiotherapy Treatment (When I felt like giving up)

CHAPTER 6

ALL WORKING TOGETHER FOR GOOD

Remember what happened long ago; acknowledge that I alone am God and that there is no one else like me. From the beginning I predicted the outcome; long ago I foretold what would happen. I said that my plans would never fail, that I would do everything I intended to do
(Isa 46: 9-10 GNB).

THANKFUL FOR THE THINGS HE'S BROUGHT ME THROUGH

One reason that motivated me to make the effort to put this account together was to assure everyone who would have any reason to read this book that sometimes, very difficult experiences in the lives of believers are intended to lead them into the perfect will of God for their lives. As I explained in the introduction to this narrative, Romans 8:28 says *'And we know that all things work together for good to them that love God, to them who are the called according to His purpose'.* This is particularly so for the children of God, who live in obedience and in righteousness, and prayerfully put their trust in The Lord through faith.

The experiences in my life, which led me to make the decision to resign from my profession as a Research Scientist; a job I had very much enjoyed for many years, to become a full time minister of the gospel, has made this truth abundantly real to me. I find great fulfilment in what I do today and I thank God daily for my life. However, as this account demonstrates, my life today was birthed through the biggest storm I have so far experienced in my life.

While reflecting back on the journey of my life so far, the Lord gave me a fresh revelation into the experiences of the people of Israel in crossing the Red Sea, as recorded in the Book of Exodus chapter 14. My attention was first drawn to the praise that erupted among the people of Israel in Exodus chapter 15. Then I noted that the praise was a spontaneous reaction to the storm God had led them through in chapter 14. The experience made them simply stand in awe of God's faithfulness and of the tremendous power He had demonstrated in their favour. That testimony of God's faithfulness was a direct outcome of one of the greatest testing moments in their journey to the Promised Land. That's probably why it is said that without a test there is no testimony.

I had always considered the crossing of the red sea as one of the most pleasant experiences of their journey. No! That is far from the truth. The Lord had asked the Israelites to camp for a while near the Red Sea, knowing very well that the Egyptians were closing in on them. While meditating on this situation, I asked two main questions.

Firstly, why did God choose the pathway of the Red Sea to begin with? It was obvious that God could have taken them through other routes that would have avoided the Red Sea. When Jacob's family of about 70 people relocated from the Promised Land to Egypt in the first place, there was no record of crossing the sea. Why did God not take them through the same path to make life easier for them? Why did He choose this more challenging route for His people?

Secondly, why would God allow His children to endure such terrifying moment before opening up the sea for them to escape? God could have paved the way for them to cross over before the Egyptians could catch up with them. Not only did God not do that; He actually orchestrated the panic situation by delaying them in asking them to camp by the sea. Was that necessary? Did it give God pleasure in any way to see His people terrified by the approaching forces? The verses below capture the panic moment I am referring to.

> *'The LORD made the king stubborn, and he pursued the Israelites, who were leaving triumphantly. The Egyptian army, with all the horses, chariots, and drivers, pursued them and caught up with them where they were camped by the Red Sea near Pi Hahiroth and Baal Zephon. When the Israelites saw the king and his army marching against them, they were terrified and cried out to the LORD for help. 'They said to Moses, "Weren't there any graves in Egypt? Did you have to bring us out here in the desert to die? Look what you have done by bringing us out of Egypt! Didn't we tell you before we left that this would happen? We told you to leave us alone and let us go on being slaves of the Egyptians. It would be better to be slaves there than to die here in the desert"'* **(Exodus 14:8-12 GNB).**

The journey from Egypt, which had been initiated by God Himself, and had begun triumphantly, soon ran into serious life threatening challenges. I could very much relate with this situation. This journey represented the prospects I anticipated in my professional career, following the successful completion of my doctorate degree and immediately securing funding for two major international projects. This triumphant journey, which was clearly the doing of the Lord, pretty soon ran into a very heavy storm.

While meditating on these developments, the Lord gave me fresh insight in answer to my questions. Beside the fact that God used these situations to set Egypt up to receive their much deserved punishment for the pain they had inflicted on His people over the years; I learnt some important life lessons, which I wish to share with you.

Regarding His people, God permitted this panic situation to set them up to help them overcome two major obstacles that could have prevented them from moving on into His perfect will for their lives.

1. The thought of returning to Egypt in the face of seemingly insurmountable challenges was still a real possibility:

The years the people of Israel spent in Egypt was only a phase or a chapter in the fulfilment of God's promises to Abraham; to bring a Nation out of him and bless the whole world through him (Gen 12:1-3). It was during the period of their sojourning in Egypt, that the population of Israel increased from a single family to the status of a nation with a chosen leader. Though God through His mighty intervention had delivered them from the oppression they had experienced while in Egypt; He knew that when faced with the difficulties of their journey to the Promised Land, the possibility of them wishing to go back to Egypt was still very real.

The Egyptians had allowed the Israelites to leave on the condition that they were going to sacrifice to their God and to return. Though they had breached that agreement by the time God asked them to camp near the Red Sea, they must have thought that if they chose to go back voluntarily at any point, the Egyptians would receive them back with pleasure to continue serving them as slaves. God was very much aware of this; which was one major reason why He took them through that path. He had to establish a barrier that would permanently remove that desire or possibility. Crossing the Red Sea was therefore expected to be the defining experience that would close the chapter of Egypt from their memories for good.

However, there were challenges that needed overcoming before they could have the courage to step into the pathway that God intended to pave for them through the sea, to cross over into the perfect provision He had reserved for them. That was the reason for the panic situation God orchestrated.

2. The opening of the sea was to be one of the most scary experiences they were first to observe before going through it:

When the Israelites saw the advancing Egyptian forces, they went into a state of panic and vented their fear induced frustration against Moses for bringing imminent disaster on them. In that state of panic, they however managed to cry out to God for help, and God responded to their cry. In obedience to God's instruction to Moses, he held out his hand over the sea, and the following spectacular sight began to unfold before their very eyes. *'Moses held out his hand over the sea, and the*

LORD *drove the sea back with* **a strong east wind. It blew all night** *and turned the sea into dry land. The water was divided'* **(Ex 14:21 GNB).**

❧ *The turbulence God expected them to step into*
I had never thought of it this way; when the waters of the sea move, it is not a funny sight. Can you imagine the intensity and force of the winds that could have opened up the sea? Furthermore, the winds that continued to blow all night; keeping the two mammoth waves forming the walls of the alleyway up and path open. The pathway the Lord had paved for them into their blessed land was certainly not through neatly constructed solid walls and smooth grounds for them to leisurely walk through. No! Not at all!! Thinking of it, it was indeed a turbulent situation that God was asking them to step into. The walls were made of constantly rolling raging waves, held back by strong winds, with scary splashing droplets all around them. What on earth could have made anyone gather the courage to step into such turbulence if left with any other choice?

❧ *Uncertainties about making it to the other side*
If even they were assured that the turbulent winds was to have no effect on them, remember this was not a narrow stream; it was the sea. They had no idea how long it was going to take them to go through to the other side. The other source of real worry would be; what if the strong winds holding these giant waves back seized after they had stepped into the alleyway between the waves? Your guess is as good as mine! Indeed, very few, if any at all, would have made the attempt to step into such turbulent situation with all the obvious possibilities

humanly conceivable staring them in the face, if God had not pressed that panic button.

This understanding was quite relevant to my situation. Though God had clearly given me His word to establish me in England to touch many lives, I'm not sure anything else could have made me give up my research profession without hesitation as it happened. There appeared to be too many challenges where God was leading me to. I had seen many who claimed to be doing full time ministry work, whose lives and output did not impress me. I had witnessed several down side of ministry experiences that, I had made it my life policy never to depend on ministry for my livelihood. I had maintained that disposition over several years. Wherever my job had taken me to, I had served in the church to the best of my ability as a volunteer, and I was content with that. I convinced myself that I was probably even doing better than many others in full time capacity. For that reason, I had firmly resolved that issue; I did not need to leave my profession before I could serve God in my best capacity.

On that fateful day, however, after the consultant had explained the full implication of what I was dealing with, and concluded that any treatment they were proposing for me was only to give me a 'chance' to live; the job I had so dearly clinged onto, meant nothing to me anymore. That was the defining moment that totally changed the course of my life and my priorities. I made the decision that if God gave me another chance to live; I was going to use every breath in me to serve Him in any capacity He would want me to. My job was no longer going to determine where and to what extent I could serve my God.

Indeed, sometimes the challenges of where God is leading us to could prevent us from taking that bold step into His will; but thank God, He knows when we are struggling with His guidance. He knows when our capacity does not match up to the test. In such moments, our loving God steps in to help us in our weaknesses. He provides a way to help us scale seemingly insurmountable walls. When it becomes overwhelming, The Lord provides a way of escape (1Cor 10:13). He may permit situations that would push us out of our comfort zone. That is exactly what God did in my case.

By permitting that panic situation, God gave them no more time and space to ponder over what could happen in the middle of the sea, and to weigh other options; which obviously would have taken them away from God's plan. The thought of those scary massive walls giving way after stepping into it, could have instilled so much fear that the option of returning to Egypt would have looked a better of two evils. Furthermore, those with this disposition could have spread fear among the people and divide their ranks just as it happened much later in the book of **Numbers 14:1-4**.

My experiences in the past few years have been my Red Sea encounter. Having been through this scary pathway and come out; I look back with pure gratitude to God, just as Miriam and the others burst into spontaneous praise in Exodus 15. Those experiences became the defining moment for me; I have never looked back since then. Indeed it has all worked out together for my good. These experiences have become the bedrock of my strength. I am highly motivated in what I do; I face the numerous challenges of my assignment, without looking back with regret. Today my life is a blessing to many and I am convinced that God will continue to touch many more lives through my life. The following lyrics of the song by Andrae Crouch now make so much sense to me . . .

> *Through it all, through it all, I've learned to trust in Jesus, I've learned to trust in God. Through it all, through it all, I've learned to depend upon His Word . . .*
> *. . . So I thank God for the mountains, and I thank Him for the valleys, I thank Him for the storms He brought me through. For if I'd never had a problem, I wouldn't know God could solve them; I'd never know what faith in God could do.*

PRIORITISING MY RELATIONSHIPS

During this very difficult period, I learnt another important life lesson; relationships are much more valuable than possessions, qualifications or achievements in career. Having to give up the research career or the projects that had earned me much reputation among my peers leaves me with no regrets at all. Experience has now taught me that achievements, with no one to share them with, are indeed meaningless.

During those difficult days, experiencing the joy of having my family around me meant much more to me than anything else. Considering the ambitions I was pursuing, it was quite likely that I would have been separated from my family for most of the time. It has been a great joy to see my children grow up. It has been a great blessing to be part of their development at the most critical stages of their growth; an experience one can never rewind once missed. Indeed, it has all worked together for good!

Again, in those lonely hours, my wife was particularly of great blessing. She made great effort to keep up her spirit to take care of me. At the same time, she had to run around to pick up jobs here and there to keep up with the bills. She became the sole bread winner of the family for well over seven months, when I had no access to money from any source. Evelyn touched a chord in my heart that words cannot explain. I've always loved and cared very deeply for my wife; but sometimes, we do take for granted the good things that are always available to us. In fact, many people fail to recognise the value of what they have until they lose it. As a Christian leader, I have many people in my life who genuinely love and care very much for me; but my experiences have taught me that when the chips are down, it is not every hand that will be available for me to squeeze to ease my pain. Through it all, I've learnt to cling more tightly to the wife of my youth.

Another experience made strong impressions on my heart. I cherished greatly the efforts some people made to come and see how I was doing; particularly those who travelled from long distances, to simply come and spend some time with me and the family. Others who greatly touched my heart were those who were sensitive enough, to wonder how the family was coping financially. Some friends actually went a step further to provide much needed financial support to my family.

Through these experiences, The Lord has given me a soft heart for those going through challenging times. The concerns we show to those going through challenging times can make a tremendous impact. That was the basis for Apostle Paul's prayer for Onesiphorus:

'May the Lord show special kindness to Onesiphorus and all his family because he often visited and encouraged me. He was never ashamed of me because I was in chains. When he came to Rome, he searched everywhere until he found me. May the Lord show special kindness on the day of Christ's return. And you know very well how helpful he was in Ephesus' **(2Tim 1:16-18 NLT)**. *Indeed 'He comforts us in all our troubles so that we can comfort others. When they are troubled, we will be able to give them the same comfort God has given us'* **(2Cor 1:4 NLT)**.

BACK TO PREACHING

You will recall that when faced with the decision to consent to the major operation, one of the major reasons why I initially refused was the uncertainties about my ability to speak clearly after the procedure. I derive great fulfilment in teaching from the bible and I could not imagine living without it. During the pre-operation consultations, I made that concern explicitly clear to the consultant. Somehow, the medical team ended up knowing me more as a preacher than as a research scientist. It was interesting to note that even some of the records reflected 'a preacher' as my profession.

Unknown to me, coming through the two operations and radiotherapy with my speech intact had excited the team. Just two months after the end of the radiotherapy treatment, I was assigned to help out as the local pastor of the Loughborough branch of God's Vineyard Ministries. Some months later, I was seen by the consultant on one of my routine post treatment visits to the Maxillofacial Unit. After the general assessment, he asked how my speech was. I wasn't sure what he meant because I had been talking to him since I met him in the consulting room. I simply said yes, it's been good. In the course of the conversation, he asked the same question again; then it dawned on me what he really meant. So I said, 'well I am back to preaching'. With visible elation all over his face, he asked, so it did not affect your ability to preach? I said no. Then he exclaimed; that's what I've been waiting for!

When I was struggling with the decision to go ahead with the big operation, in a bid to encourage me, the consultant had revealed that he could at least refer to two professionals who had gone through similar treatments and had returned to work. I am quite sure that my case has been added to the list of success stories. In my case, however, I give the glory first and foremost to the Lord who determined my end right from the beginning.

To crown it all, God later gave me a significant personal message from Revelation 3; part of which reads:

> '. . . *These things saith he that is holy, he that is true, he that hath the key of David, he that openeth, and no man shutteth; and shutteth, and no man openeth; I know thy works: behold, I have set before thee an open door, and no man can shut it: for thou hast a little strength, and hast kept my word, and hast not denied my name* **(Rev 3:7-8 KJV)**

These have been my motivation and the driving force of my life. Since these developments, the Lord has given me wonderful opportunities to be a blessing to many; and I am persuaded that I will live on to declare His wondrous works.

Dear reader, God is real! If you've not yet had a personal relationship with Him, I wish to recommend Him to you. He says in Revelations 3:20 *'Behold, I stand at the door and knock. If anyone hears My voice and opens the door, I will come in to him and will dine with him and he with Me'* (MKJV). Will you let Him in?

REFERENCES

1. Clark L, Buchanan T and Goddard W P (2006): *Percutaneous Endoscopic Gastrostomy (PEG)*, Information for patients. Nottingham University Hospitals NHS Trust; R & R Healthprints
2. Macmillan Cancer Support (2013): *www.macmillan.org.uk/Cancerinformation/Cancertreatment* [website accessed on 11th Nov 2013]
3. Nipah J. O. (2009) The Hidden Power of Forgiveness. Combert Impressions, Ghana.
4. Warren R (2002): *The Purpose Driven Life*; Zondervan

Lightning Source UK Ltd.
Milton Keynes UK
UKOW03f0010150314

228190UK00001B/49/P